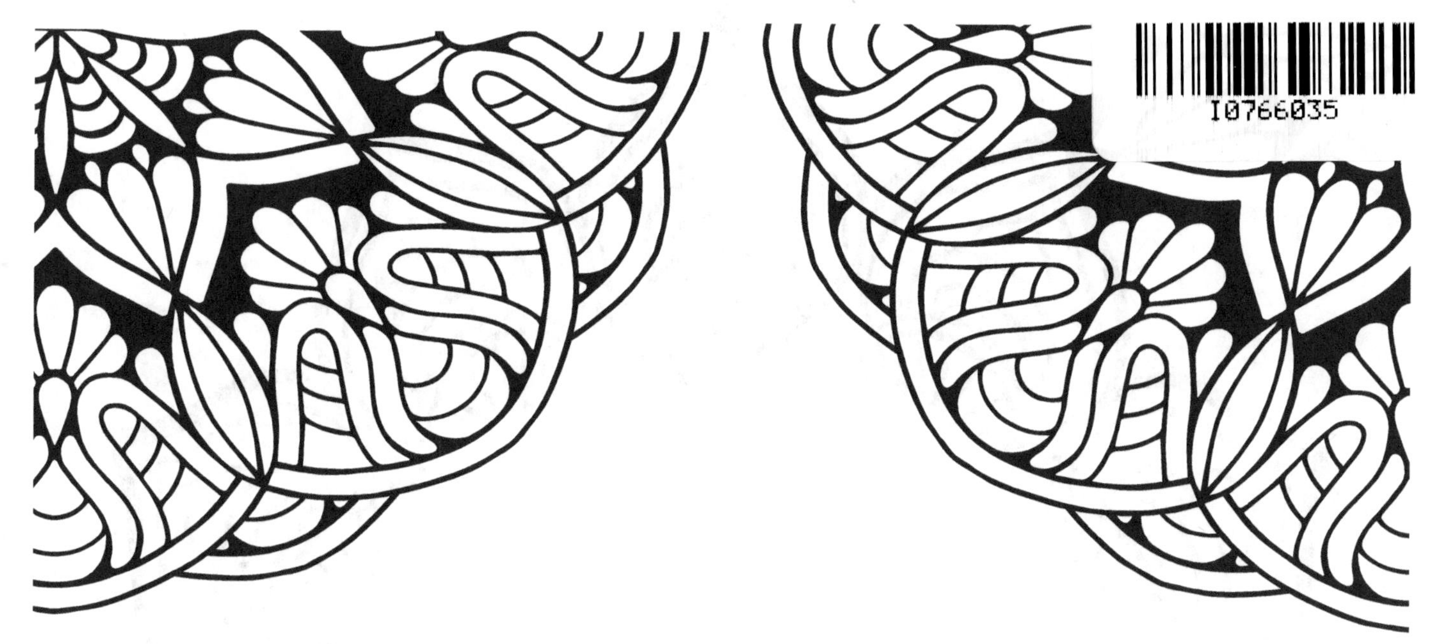

ADULT COLORING BOOK

STRESS RELIEVING

MEDOX
WAN

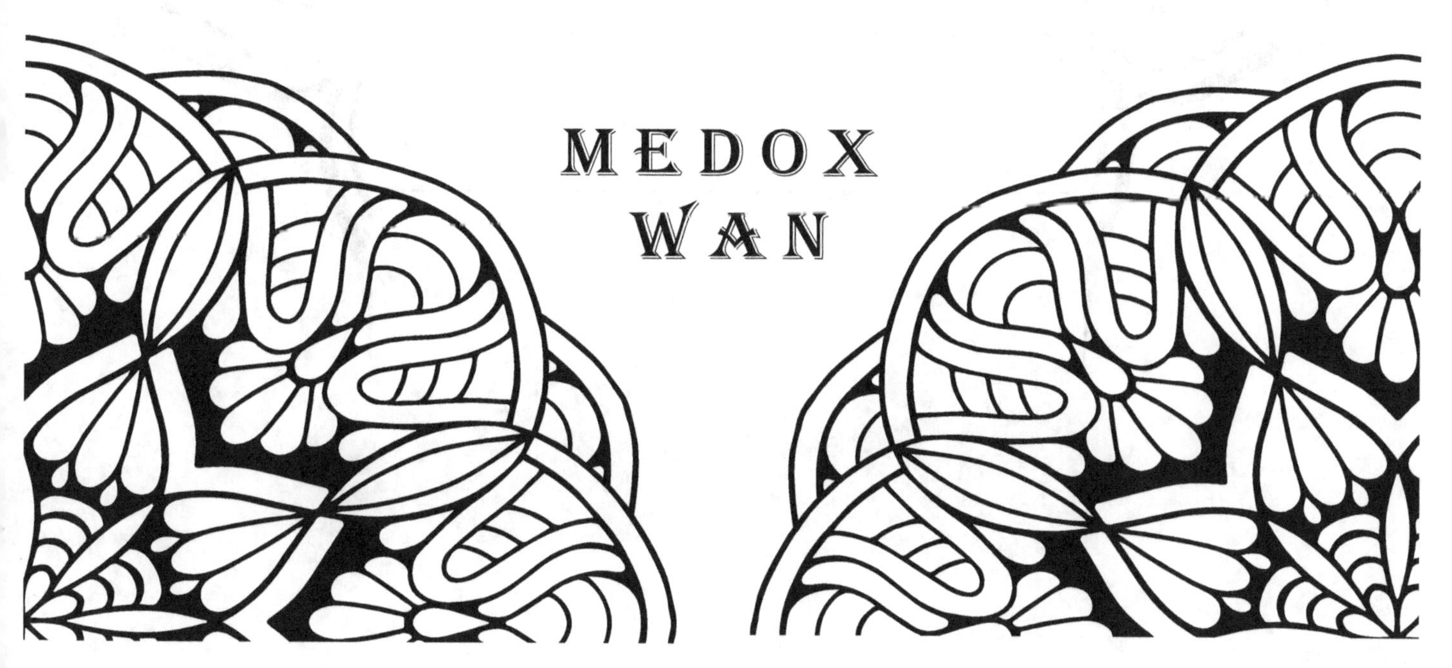

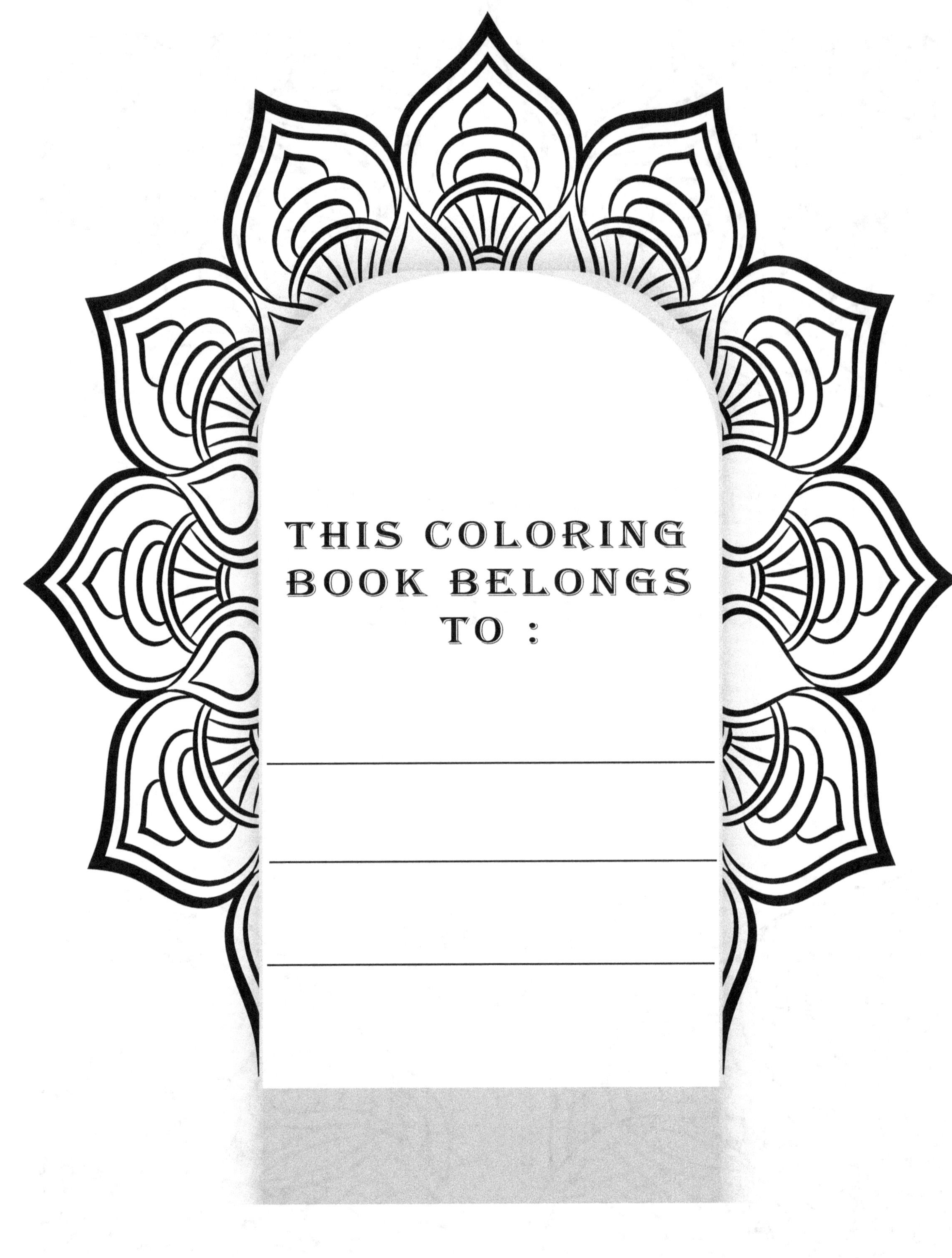
THIS COLORING
BOOK BELONGS
TO :

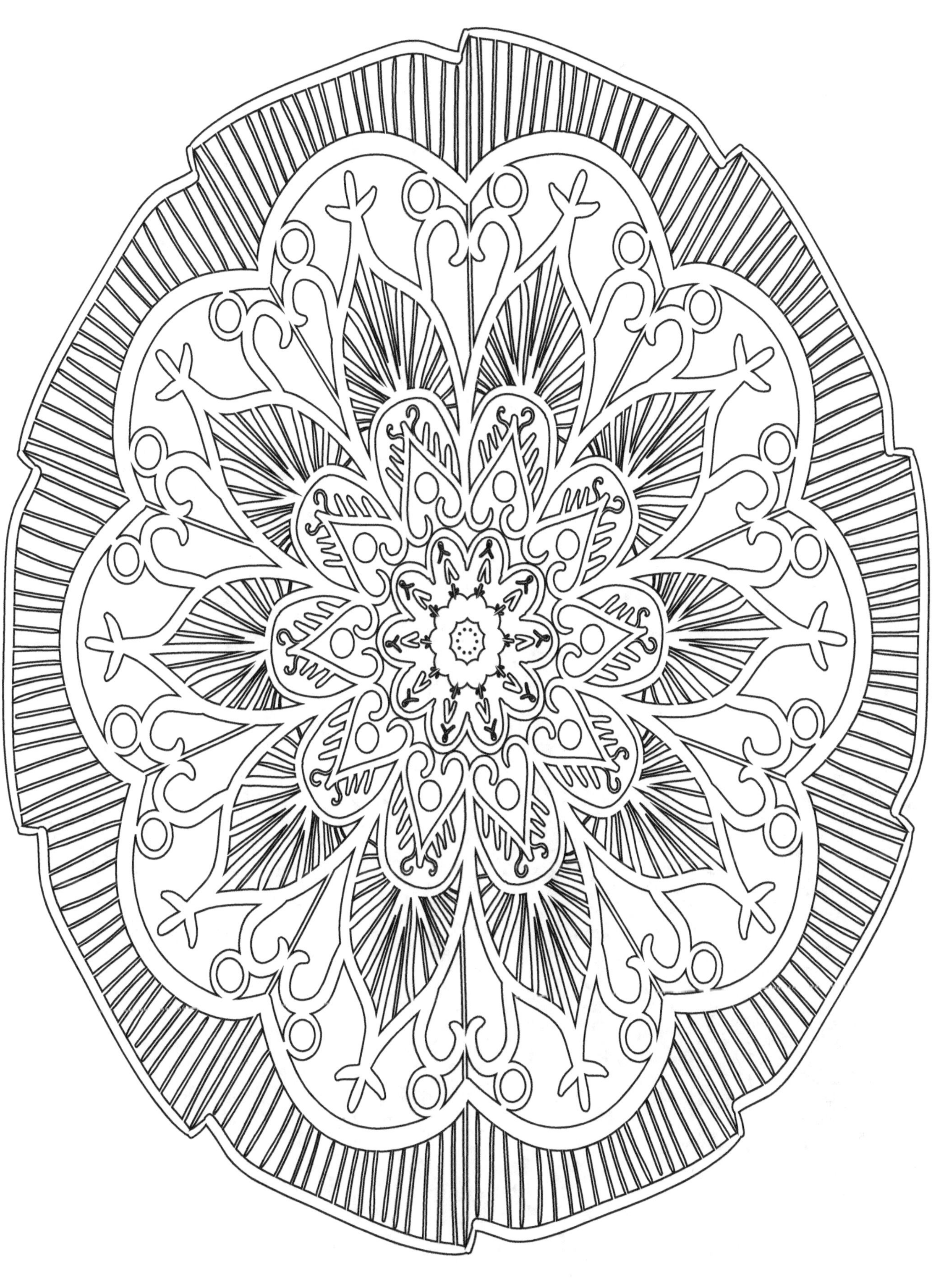

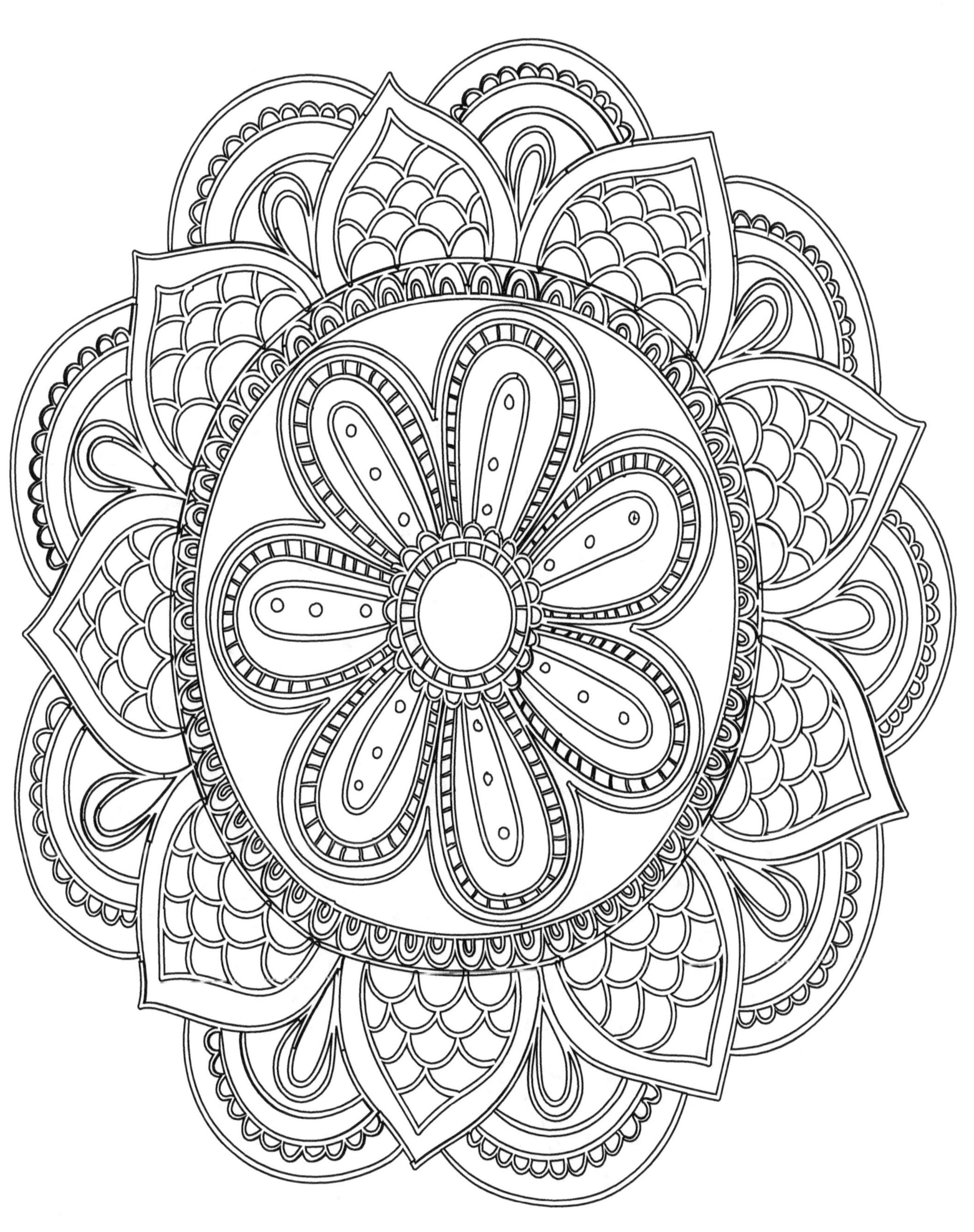

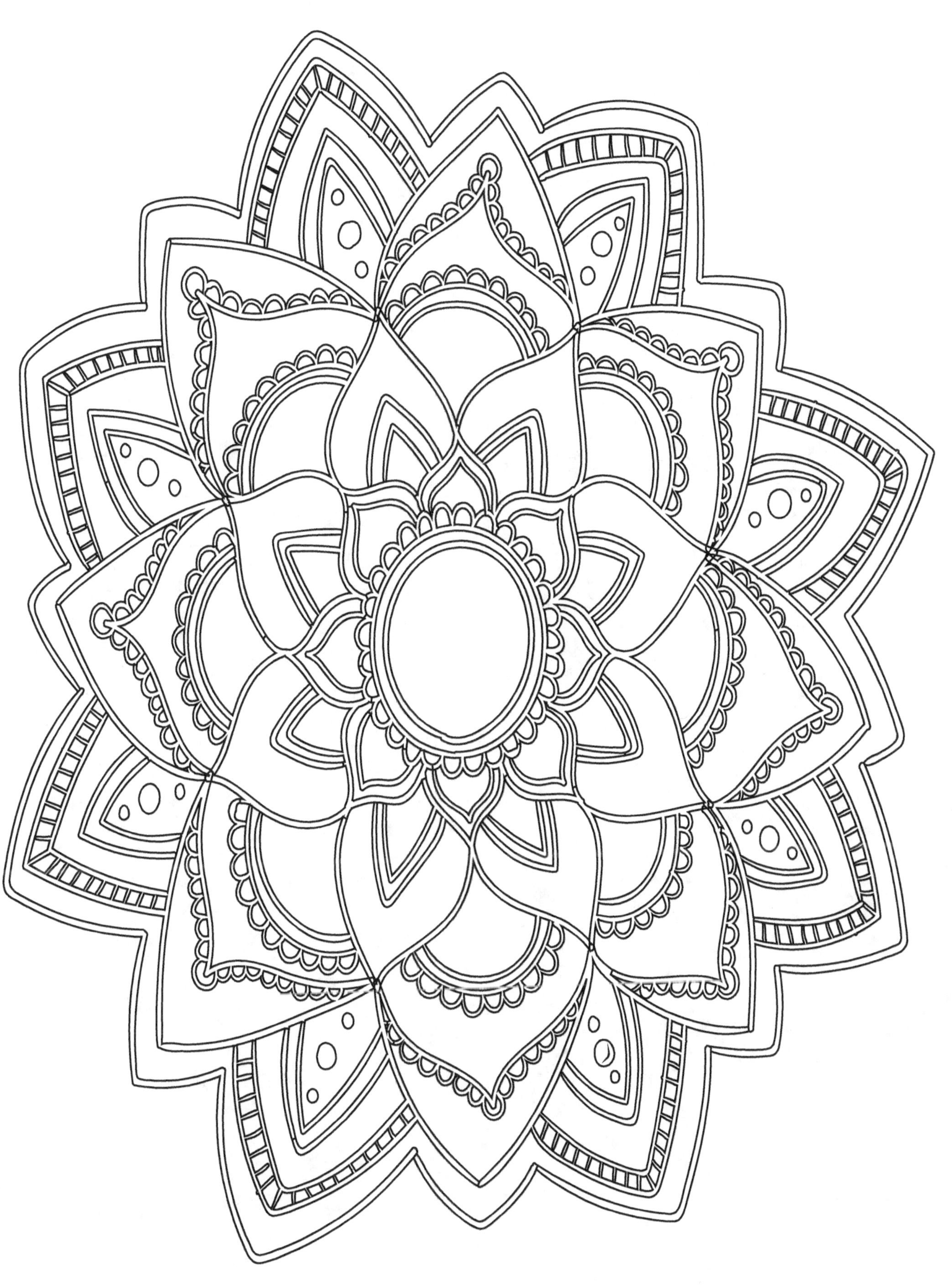

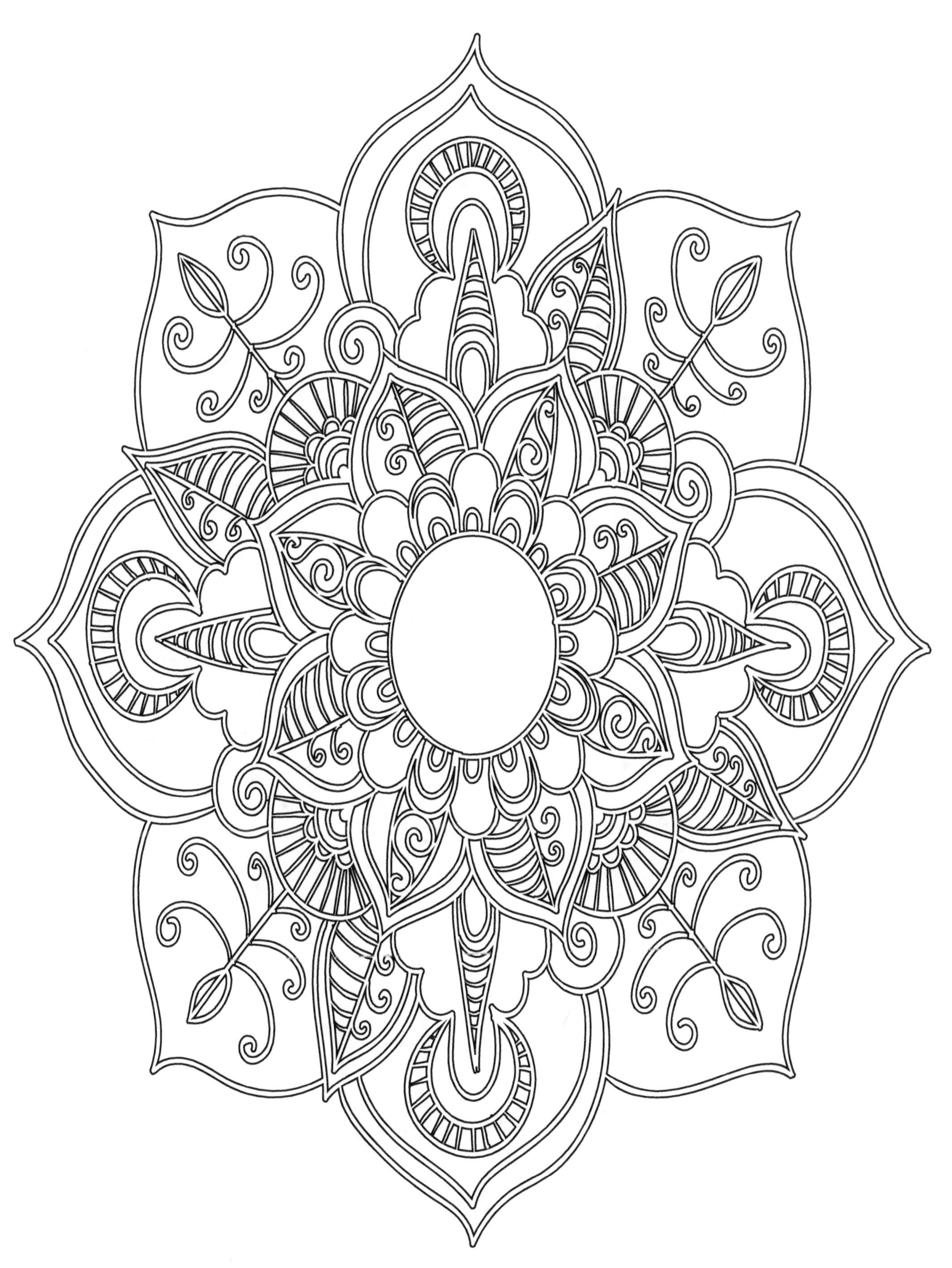

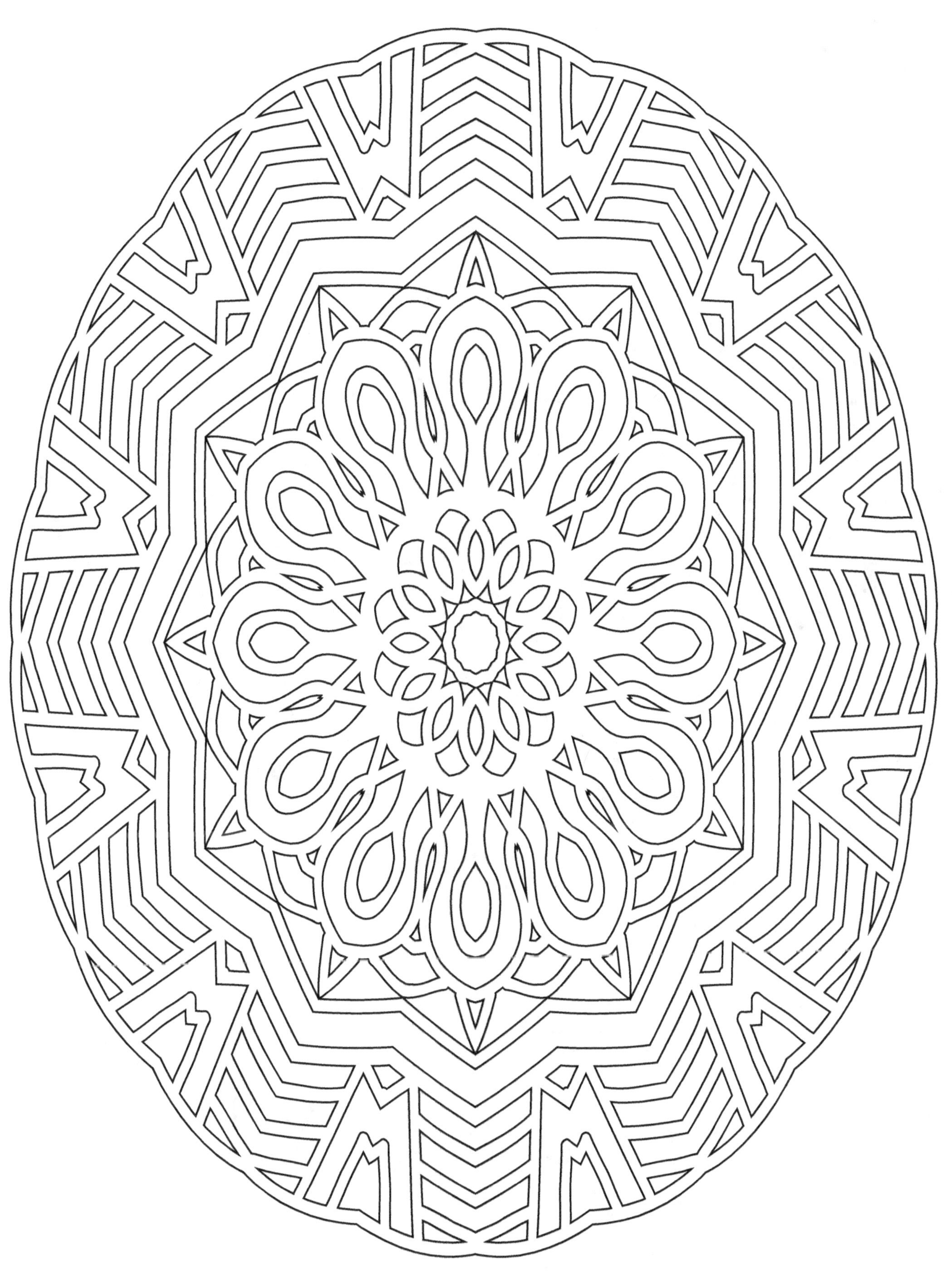

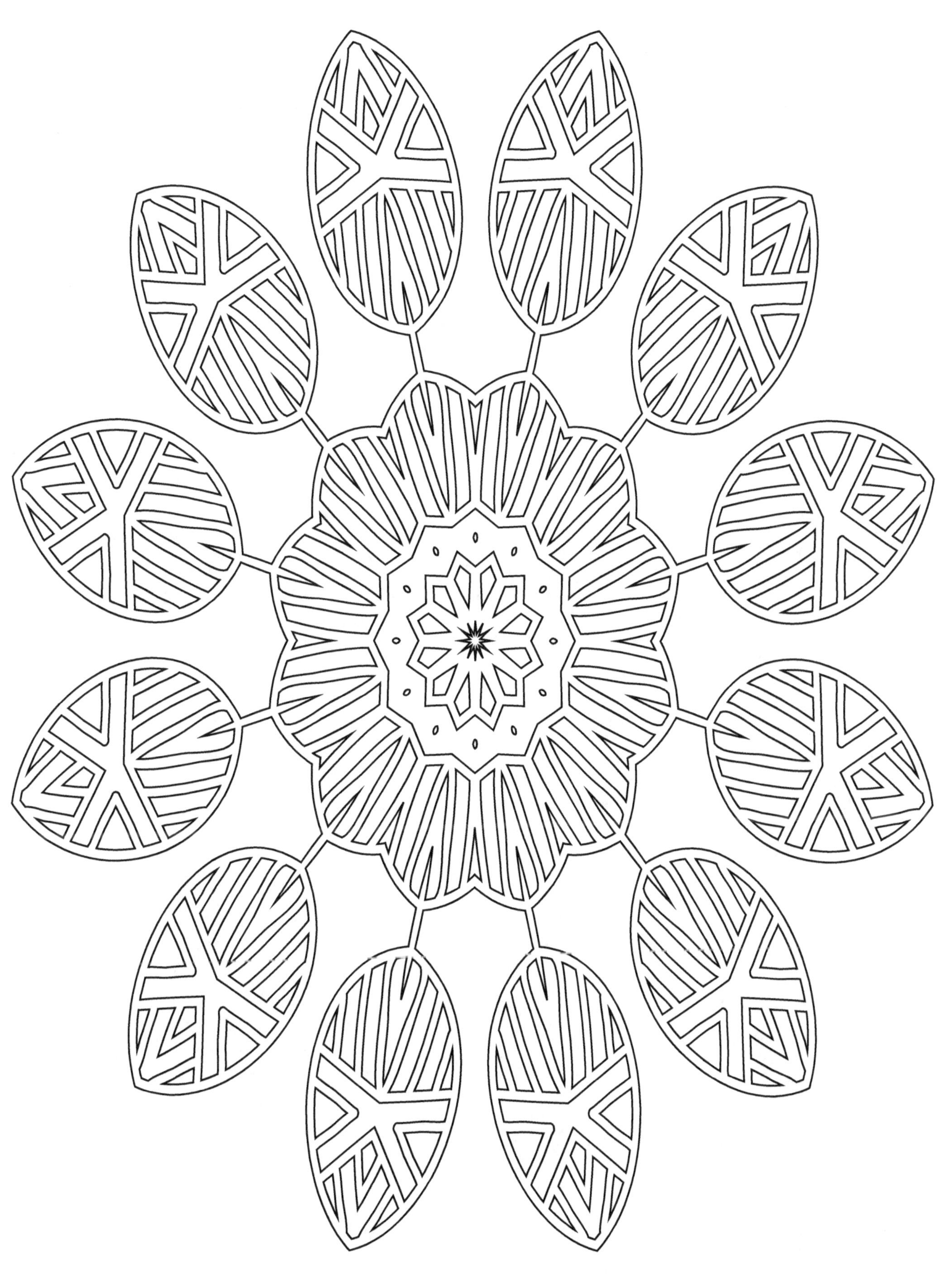

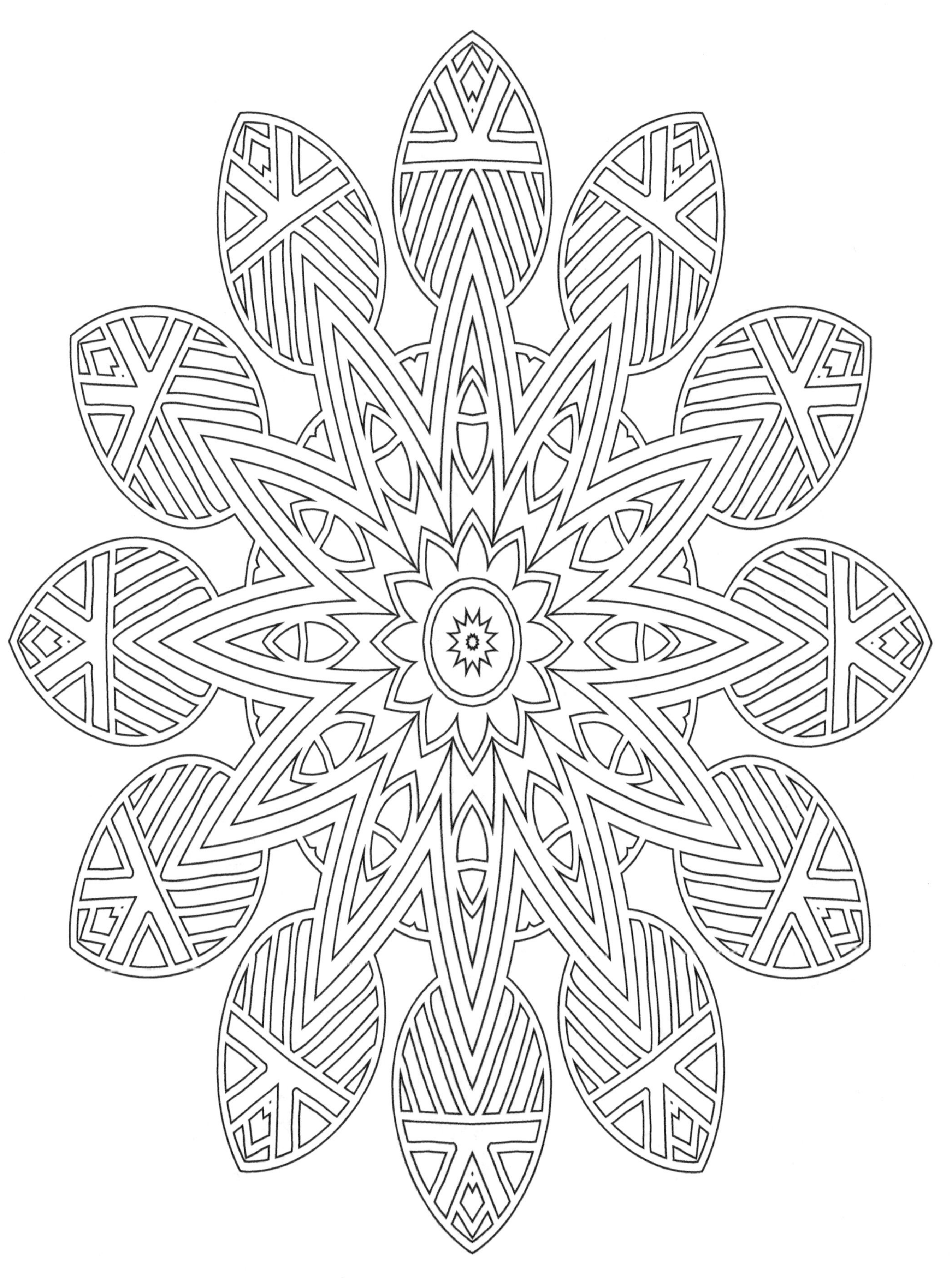

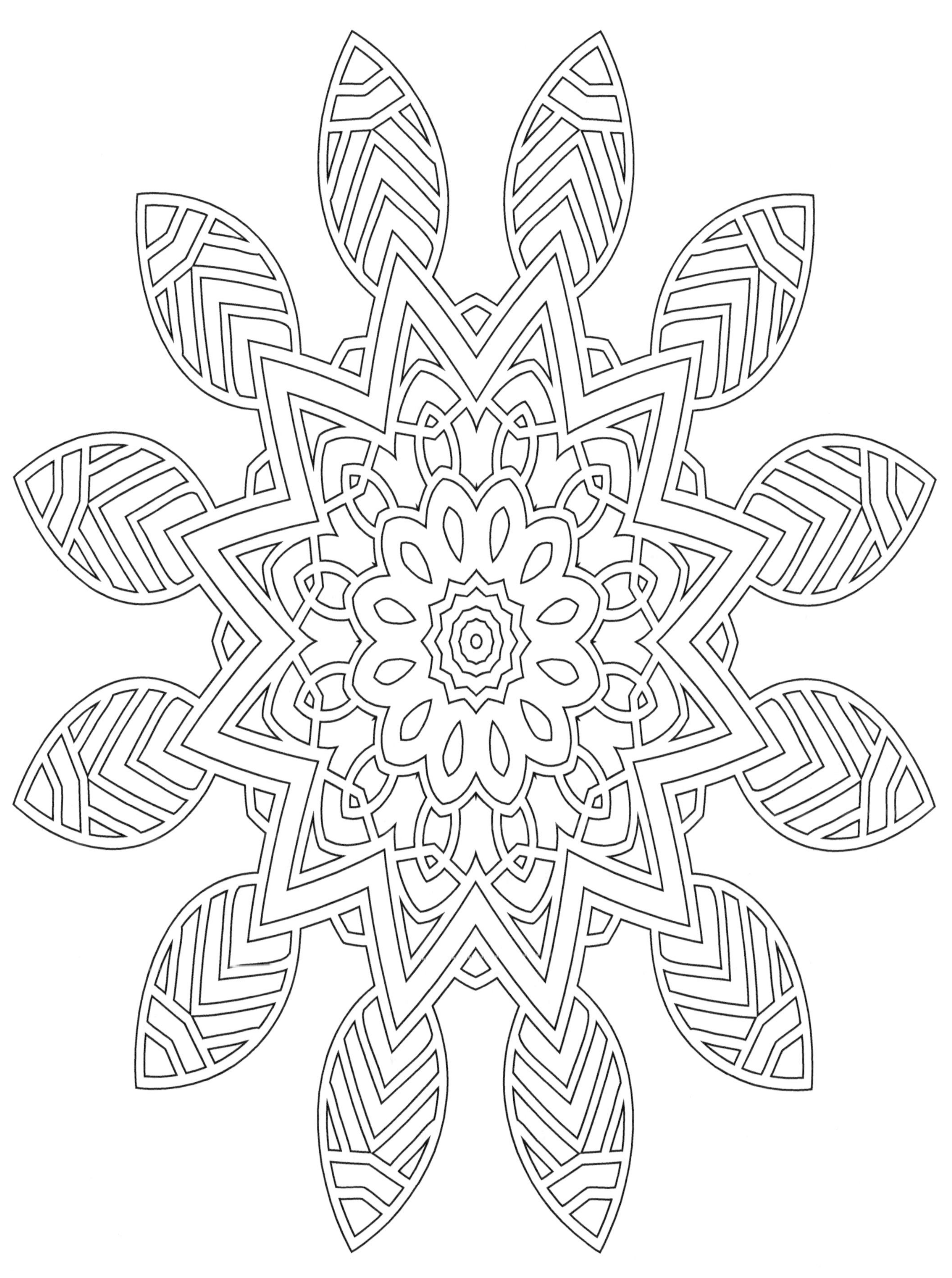

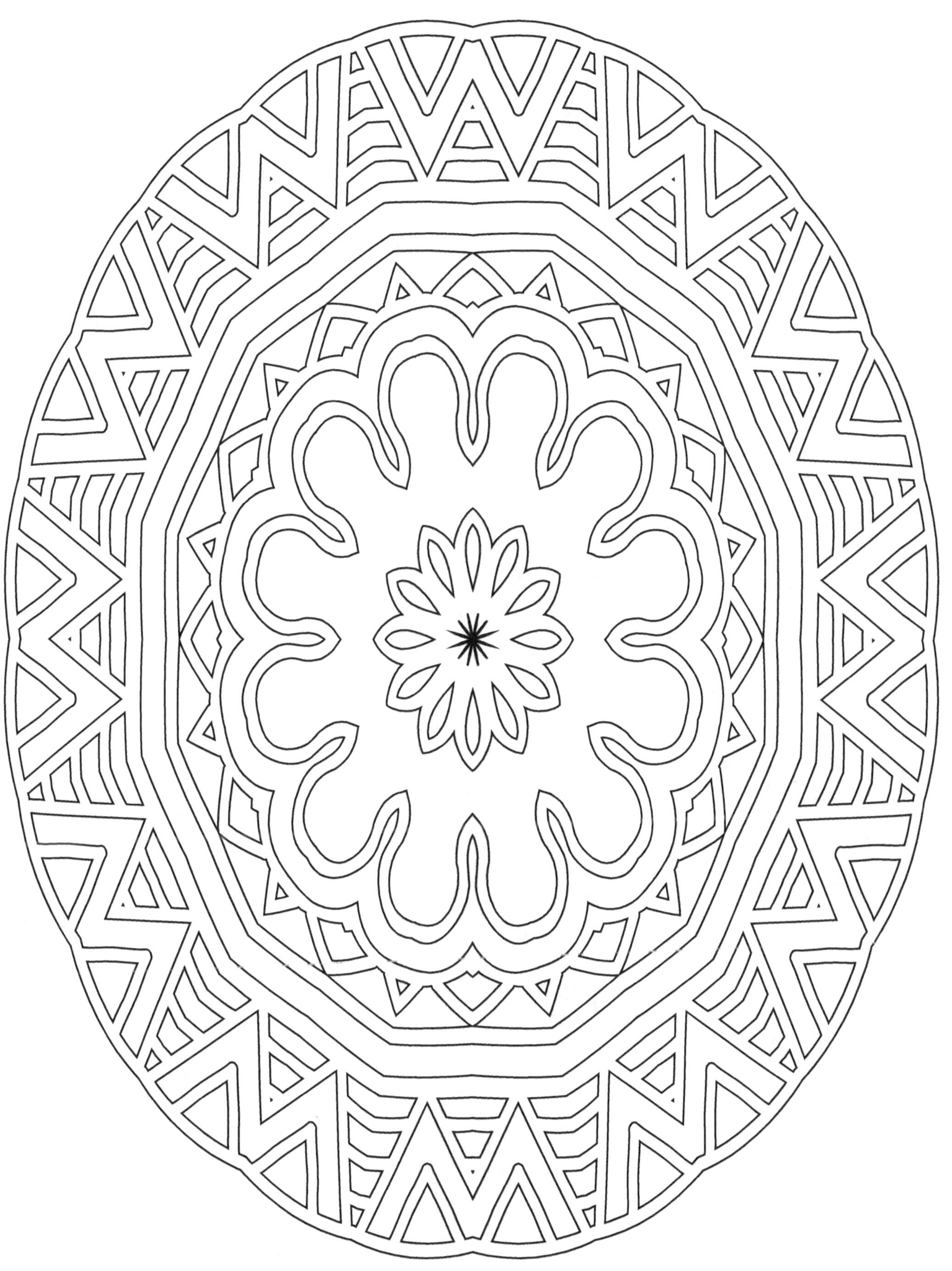

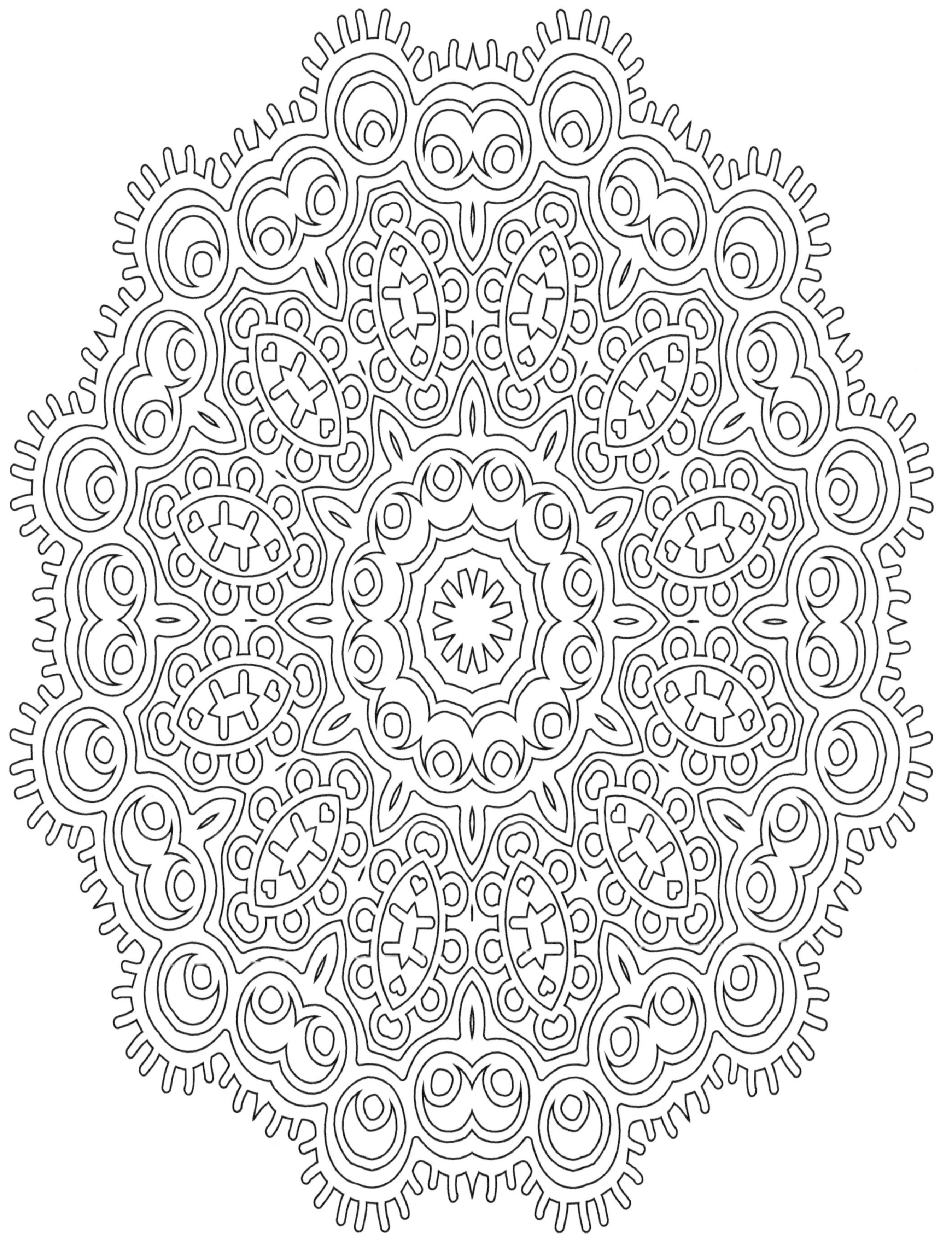

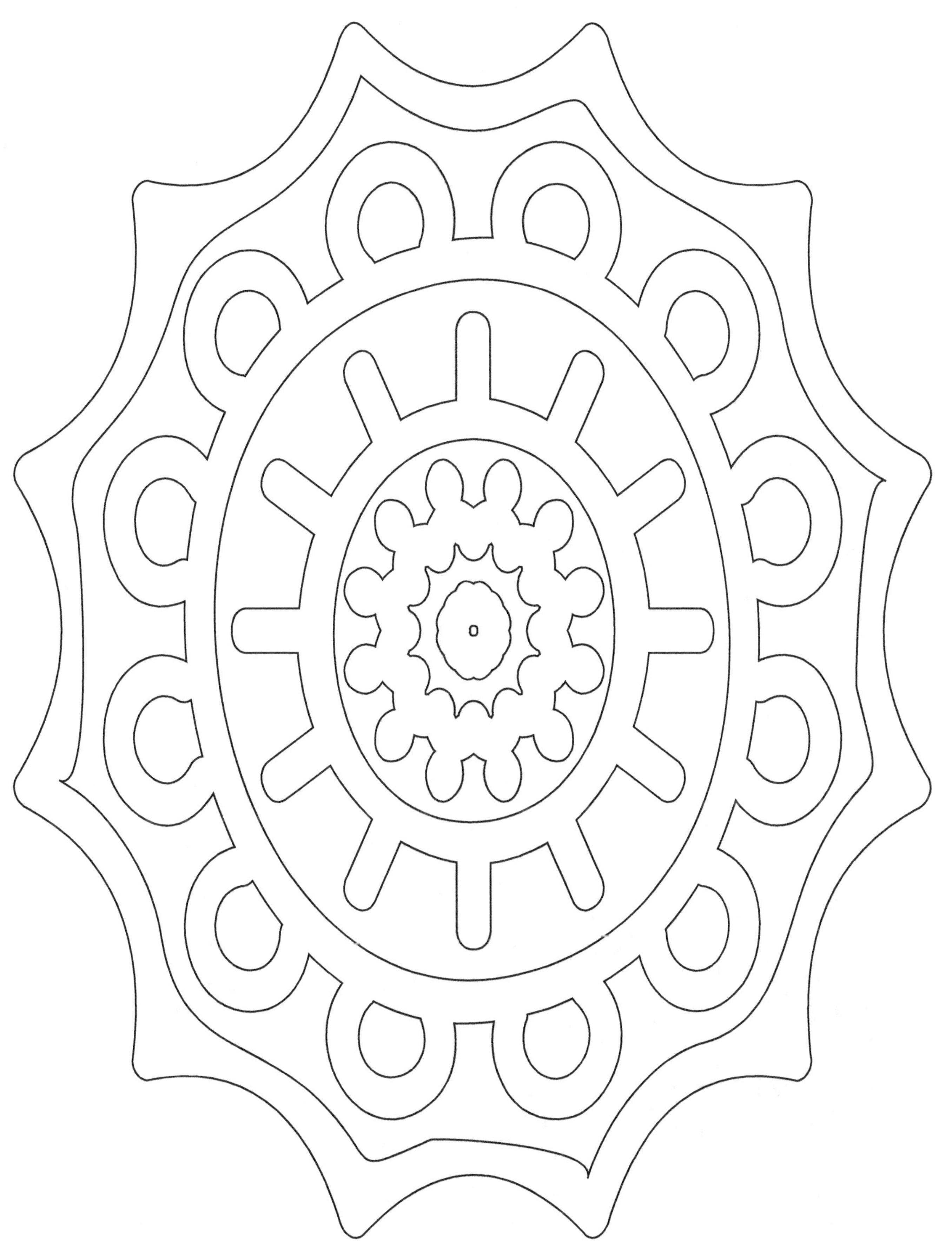

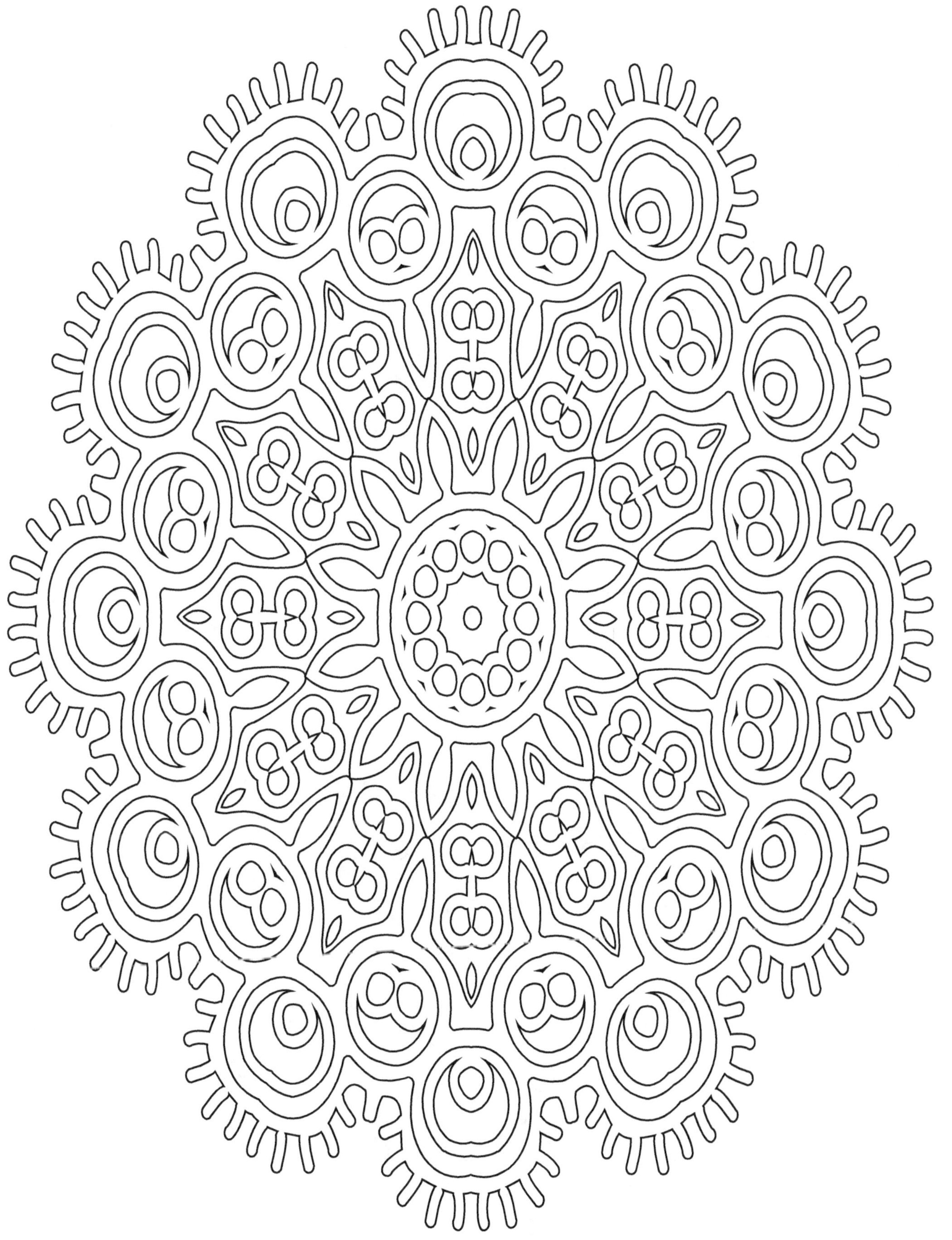

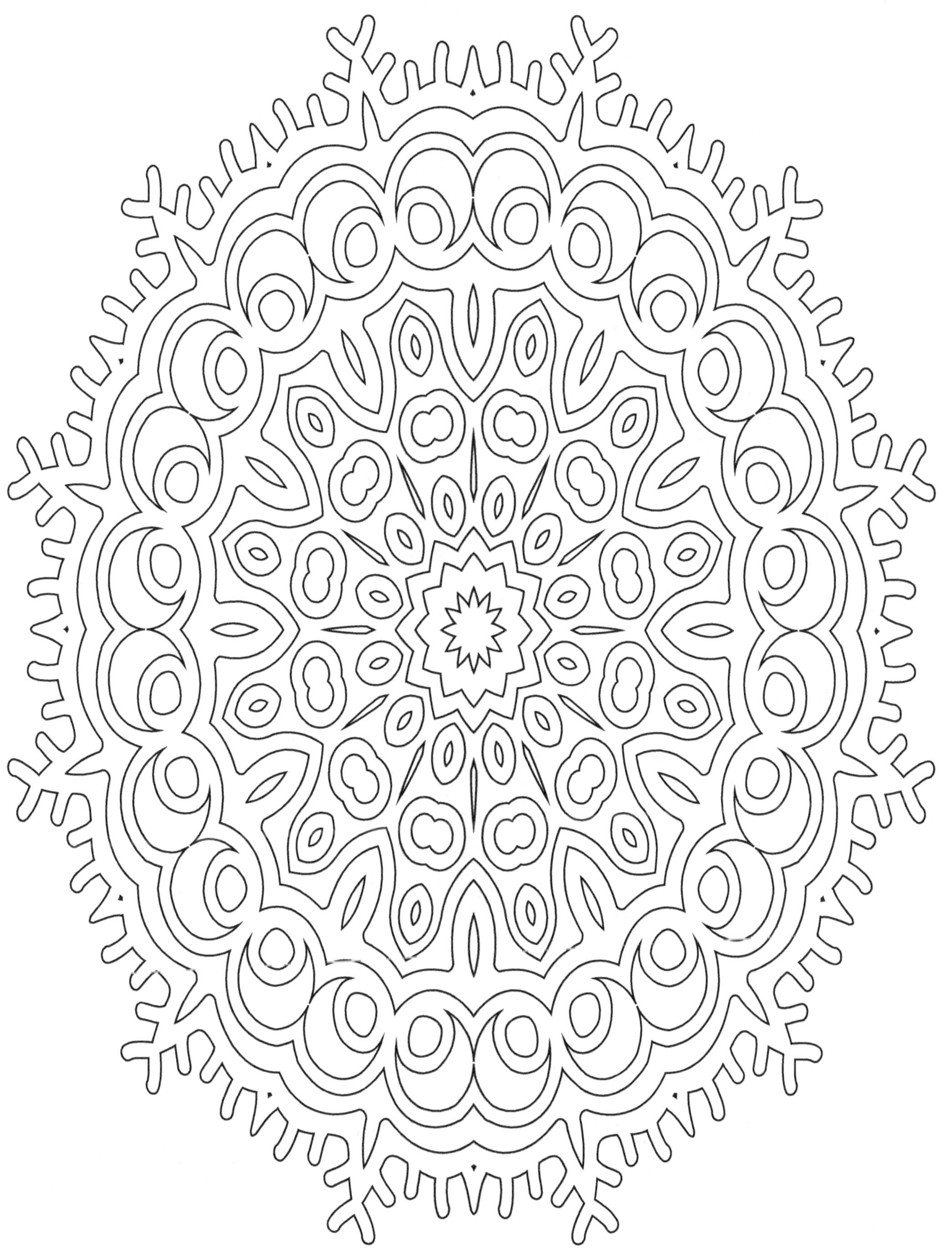

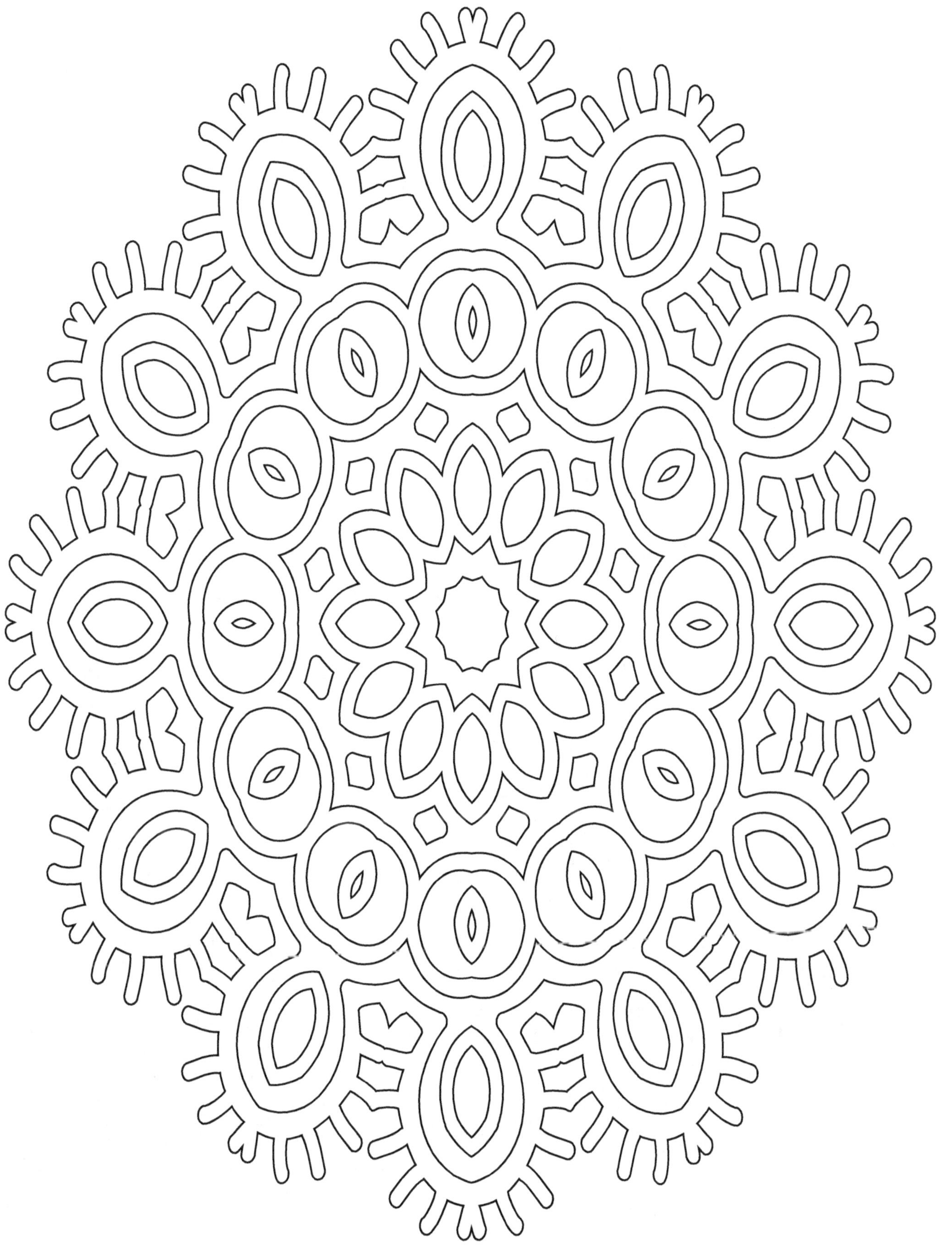

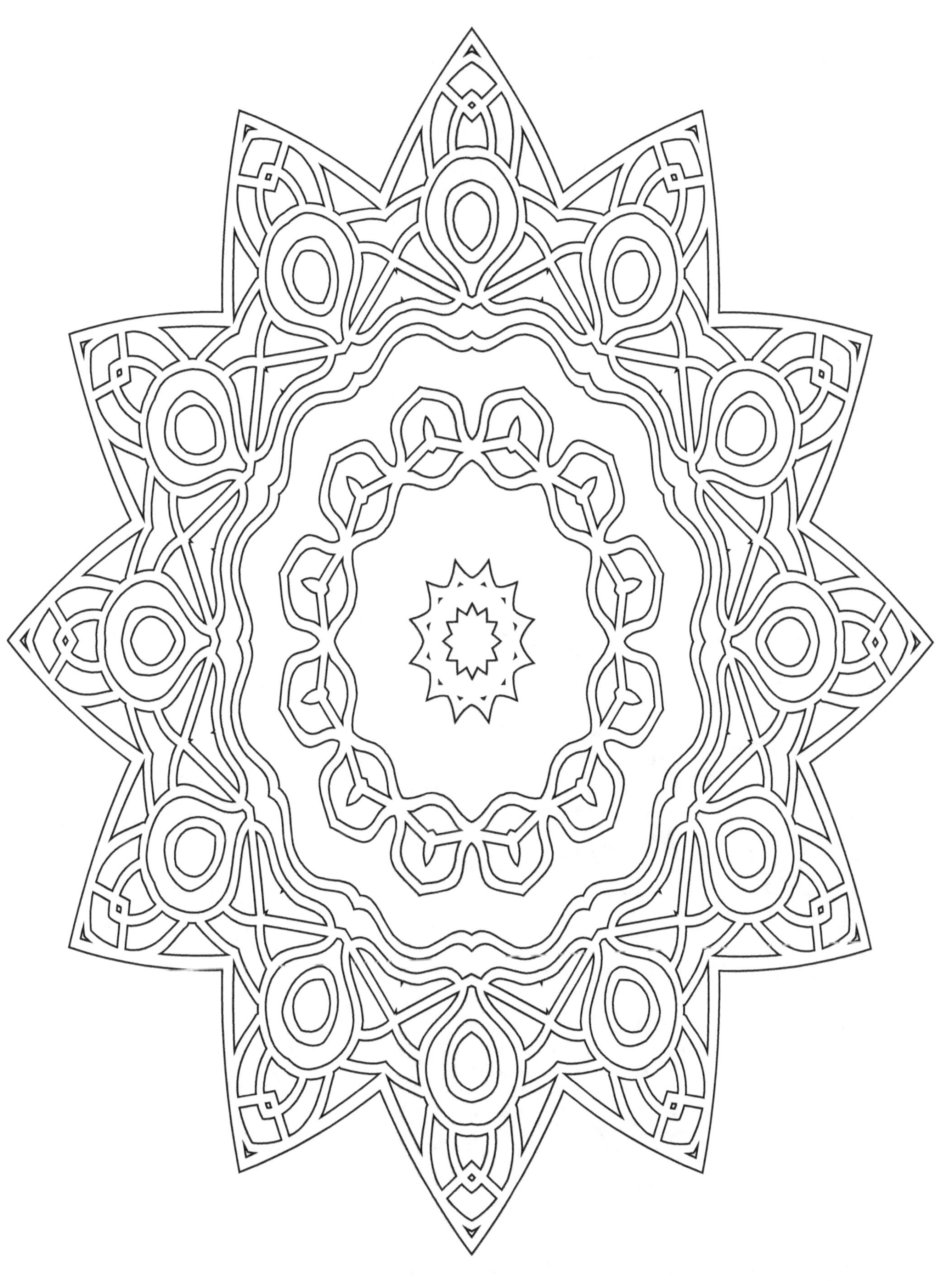

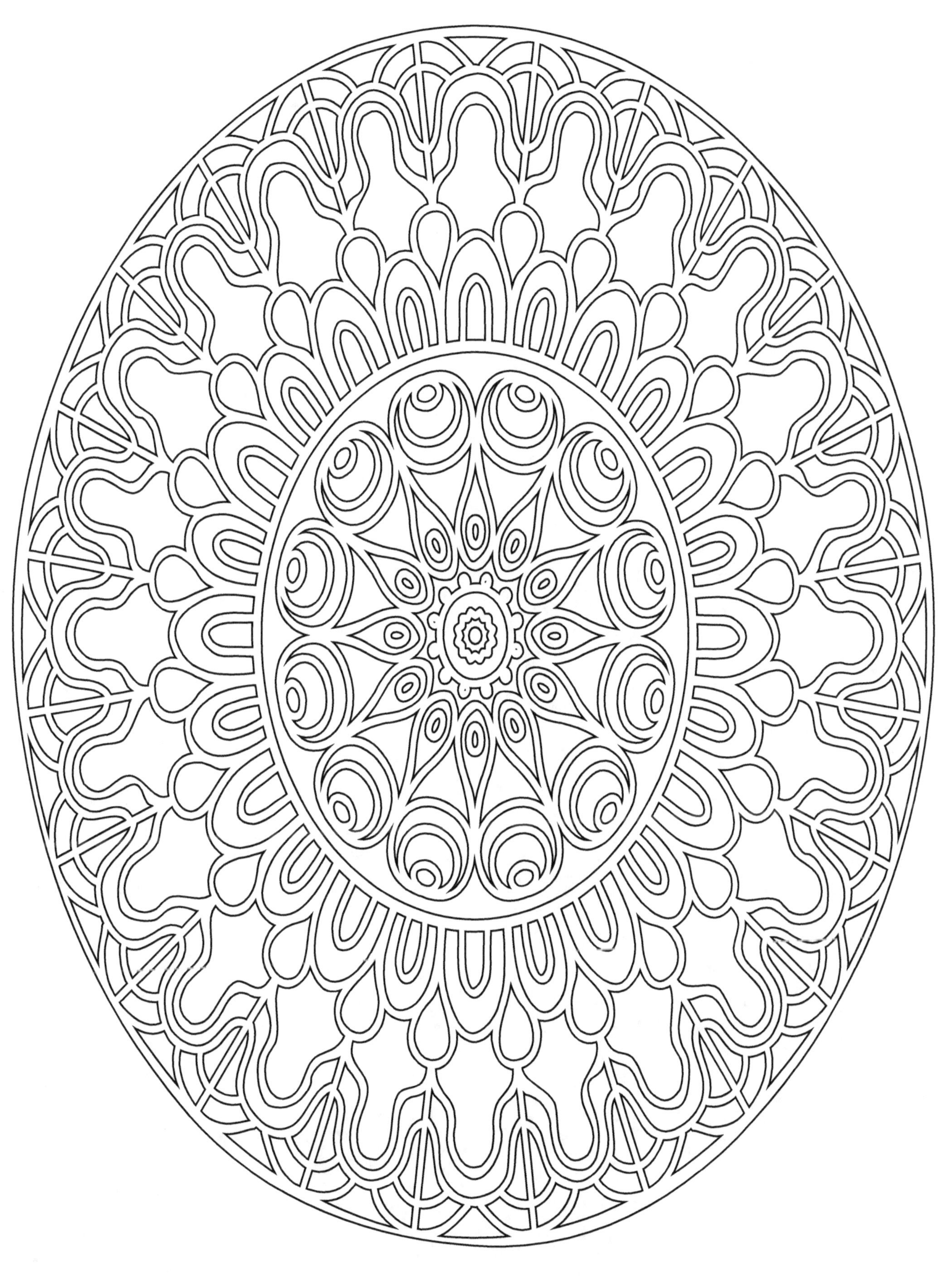

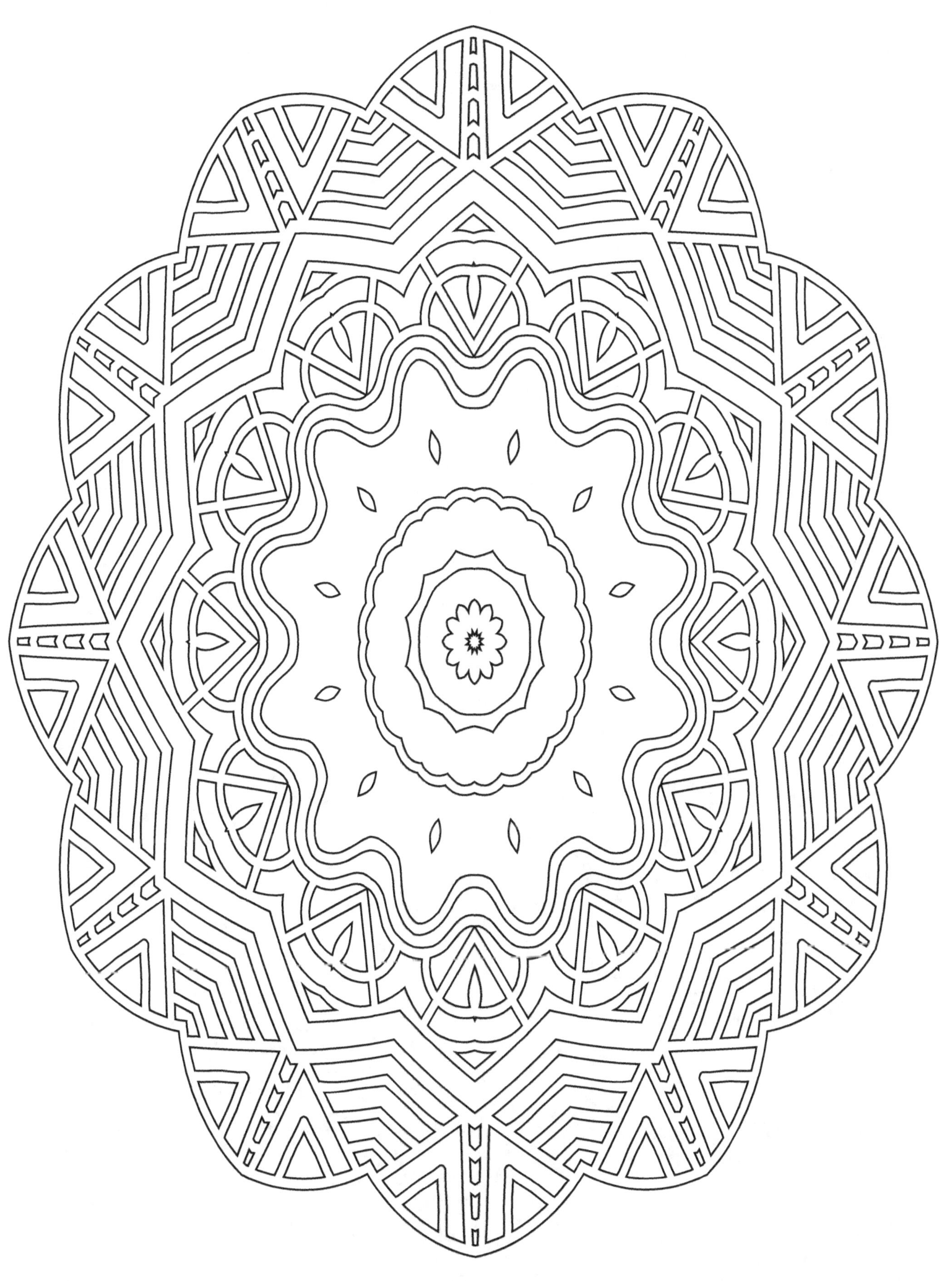

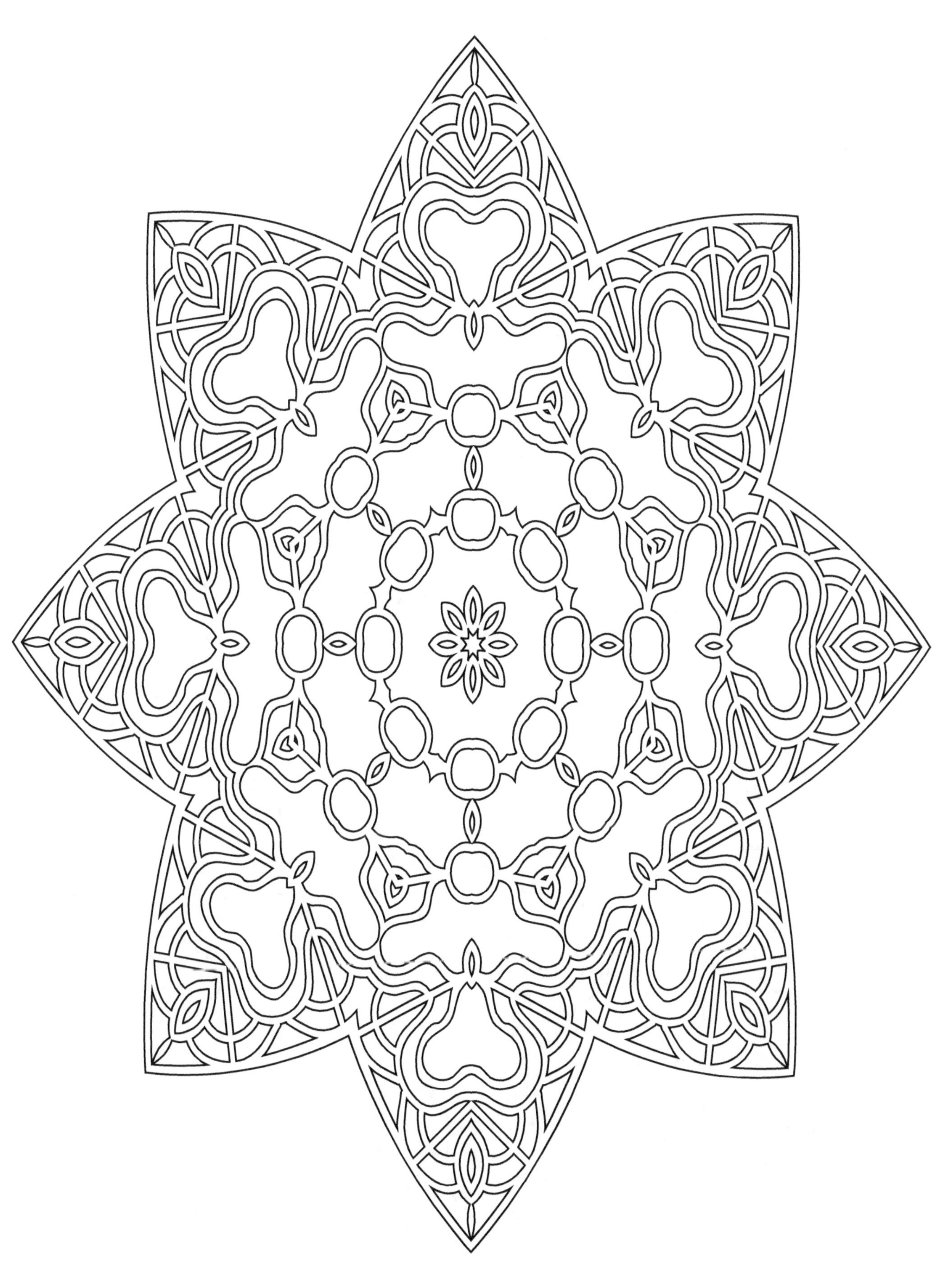

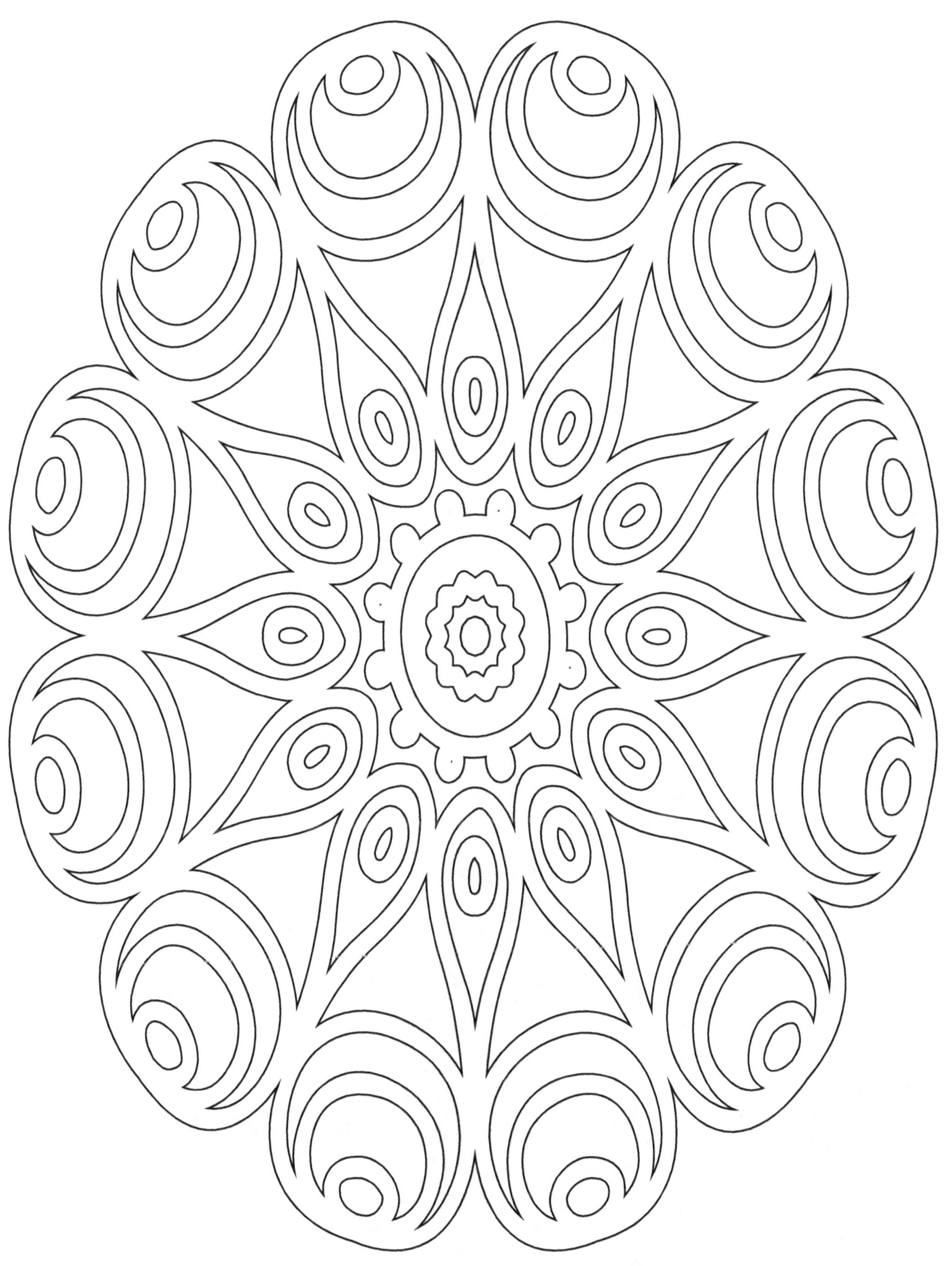

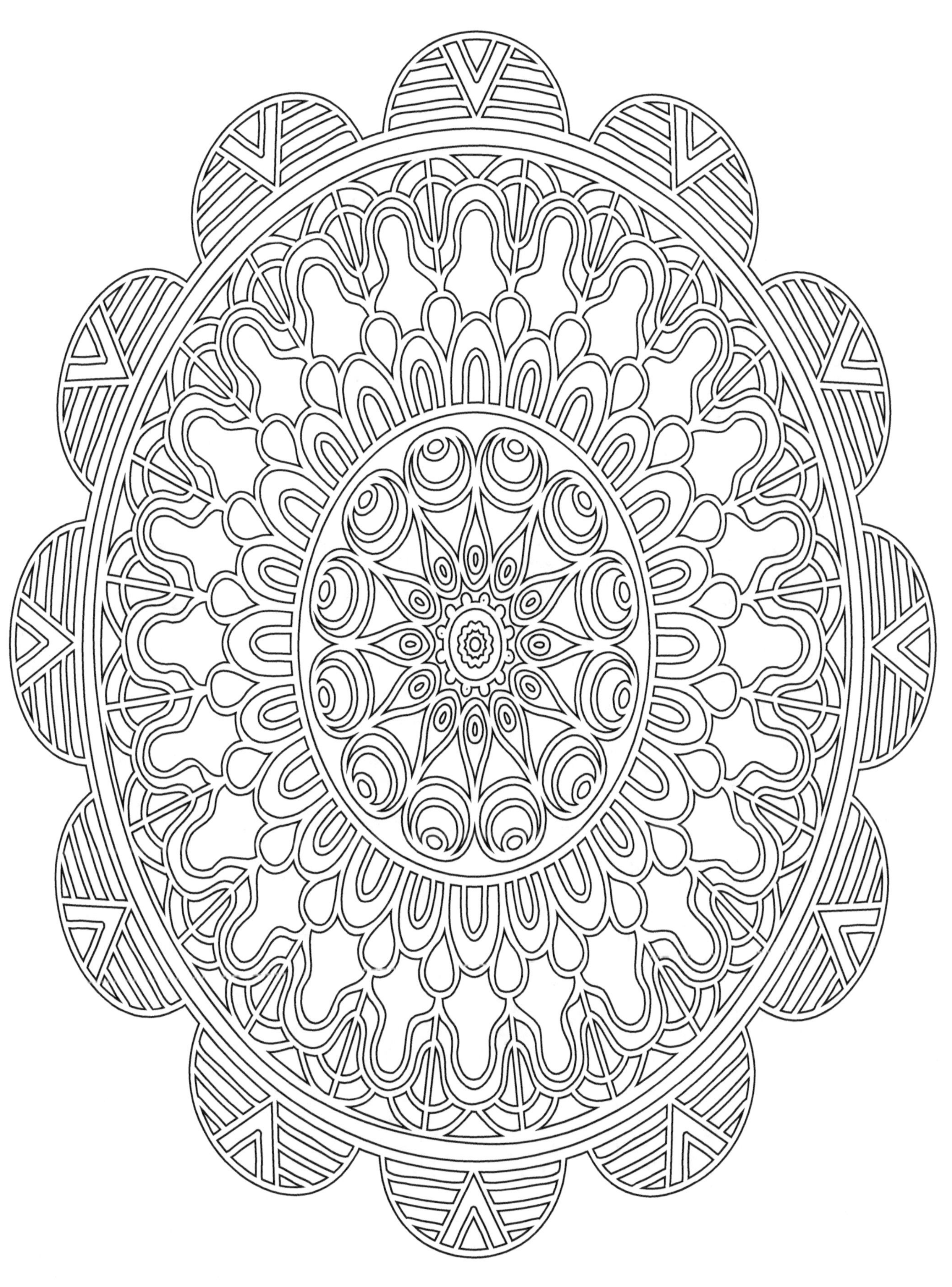

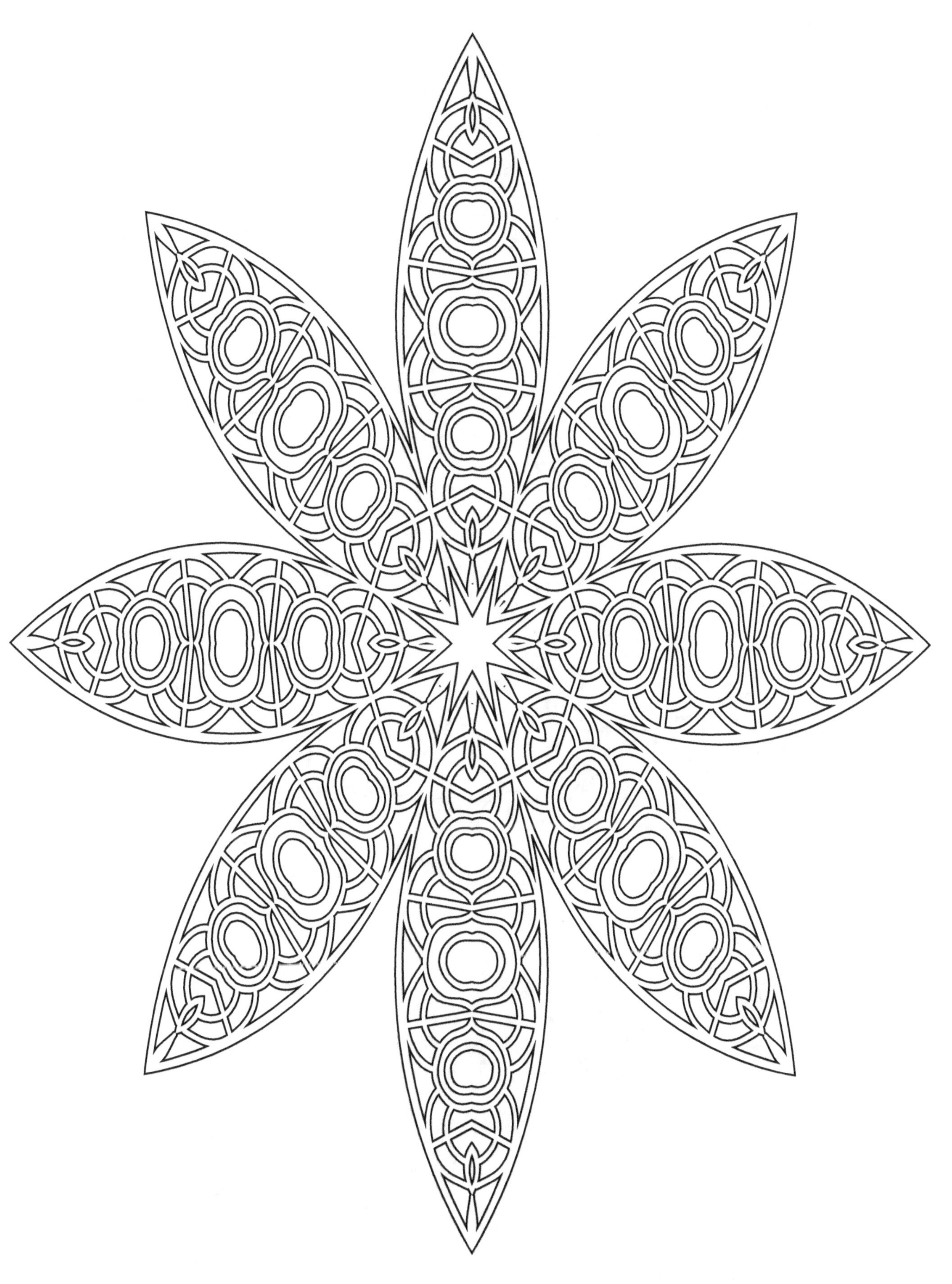

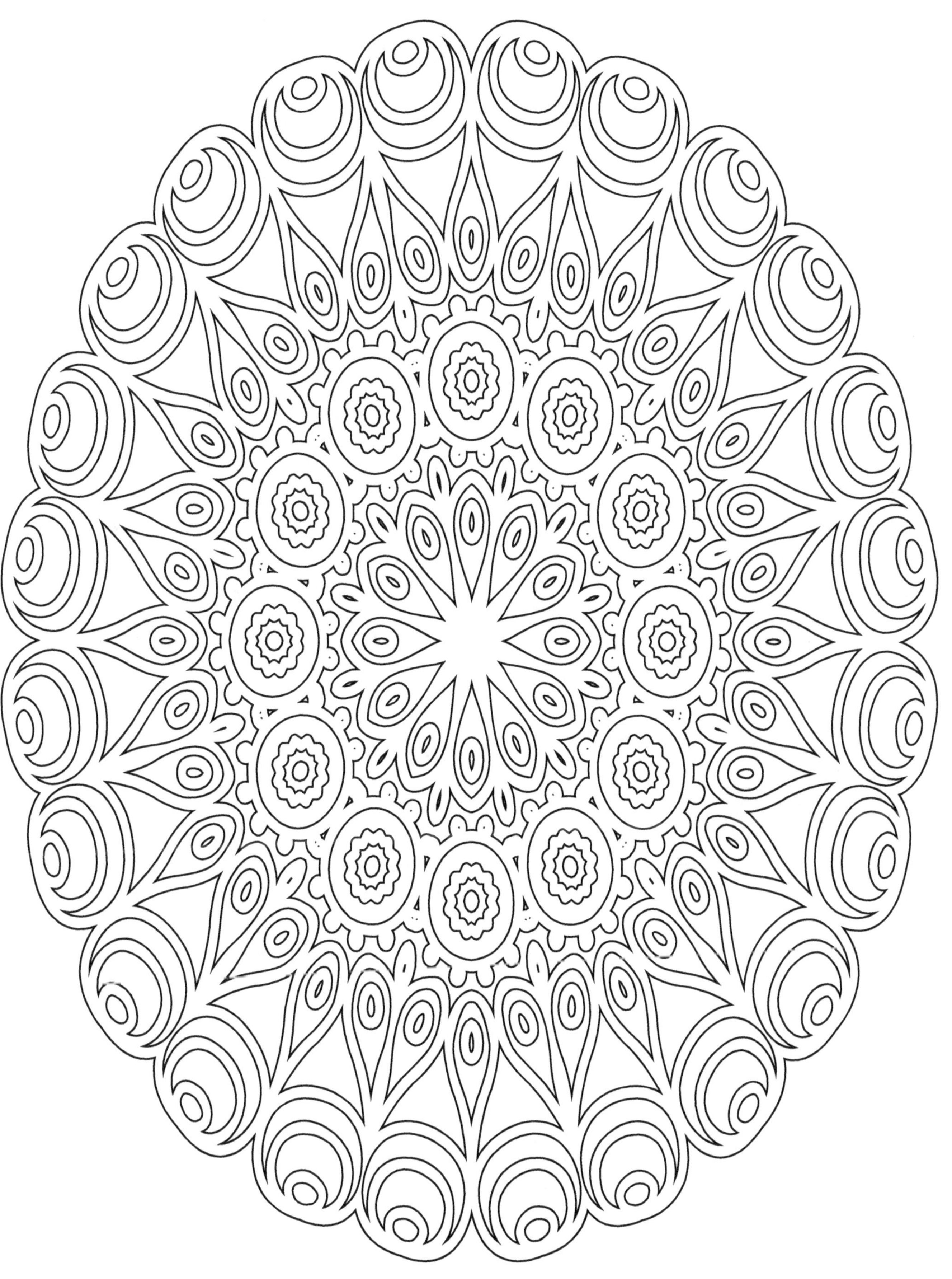

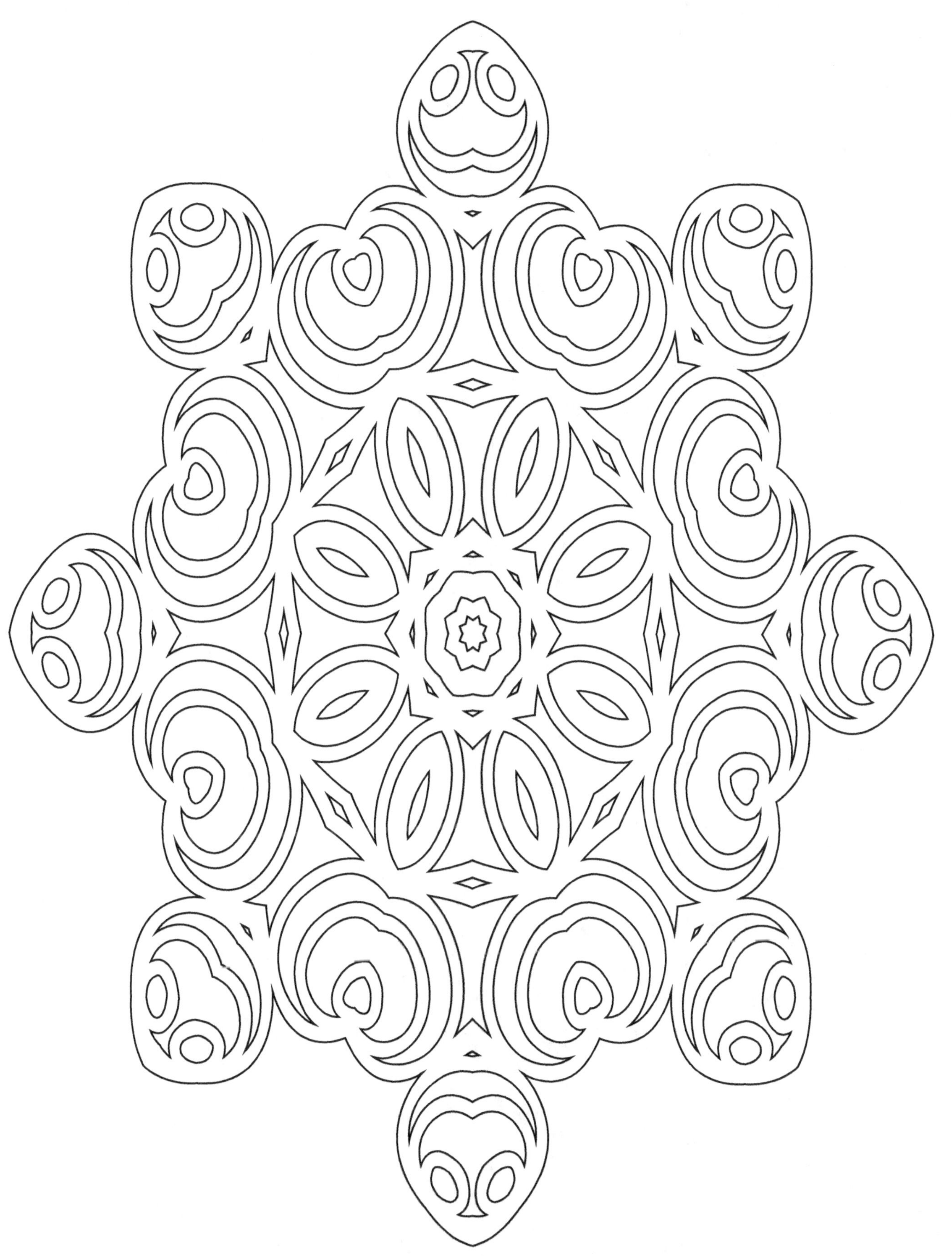

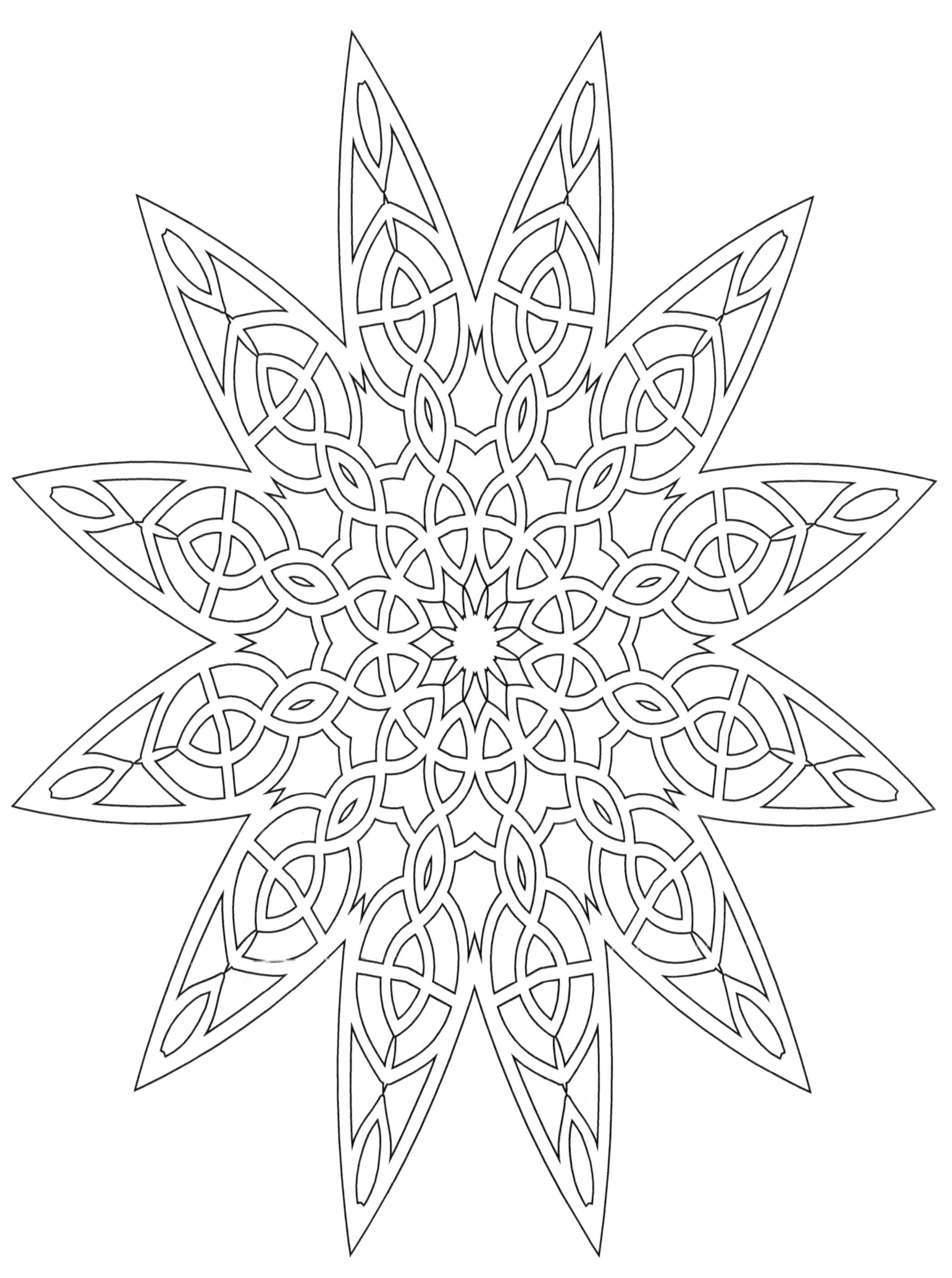

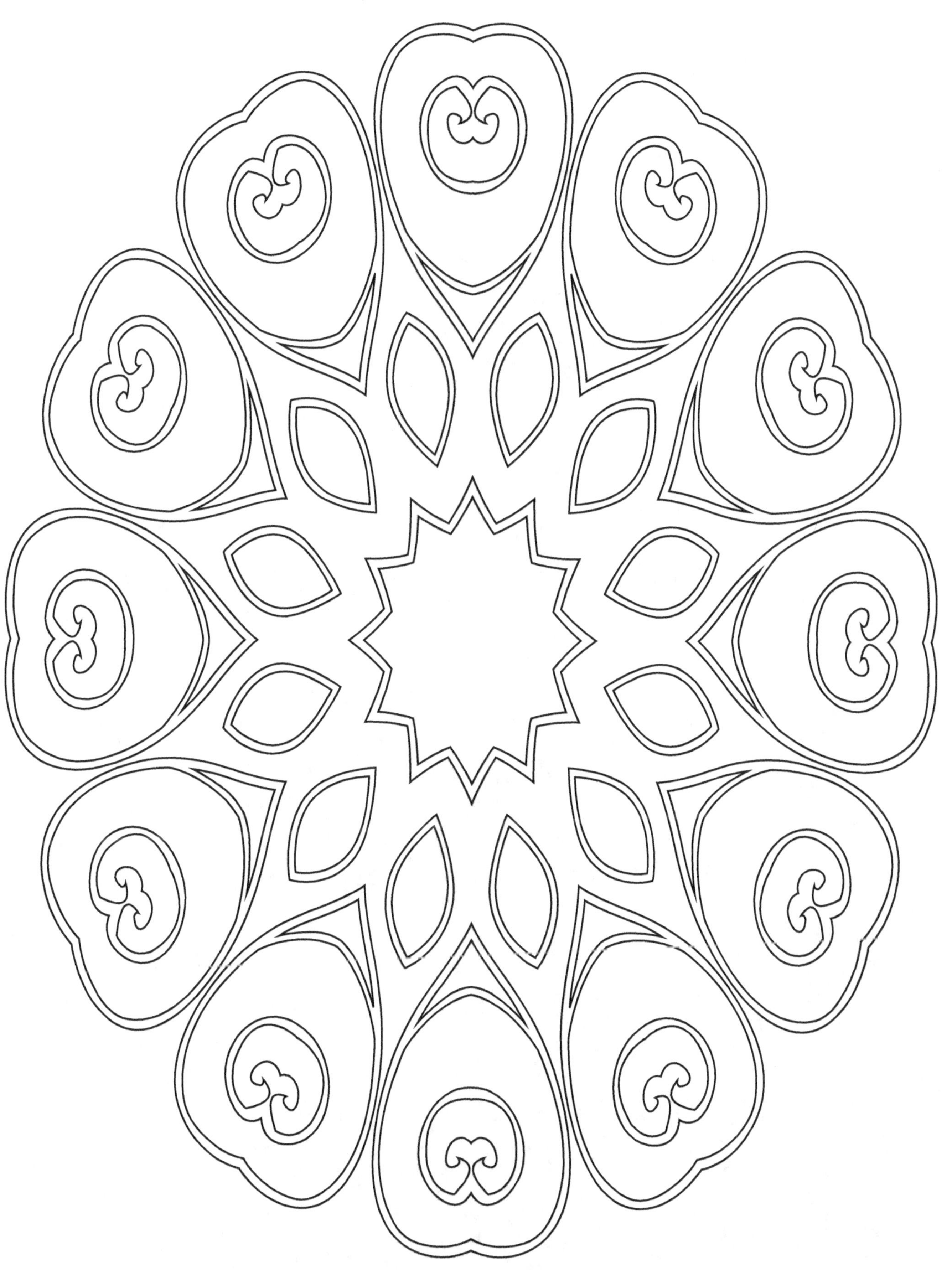

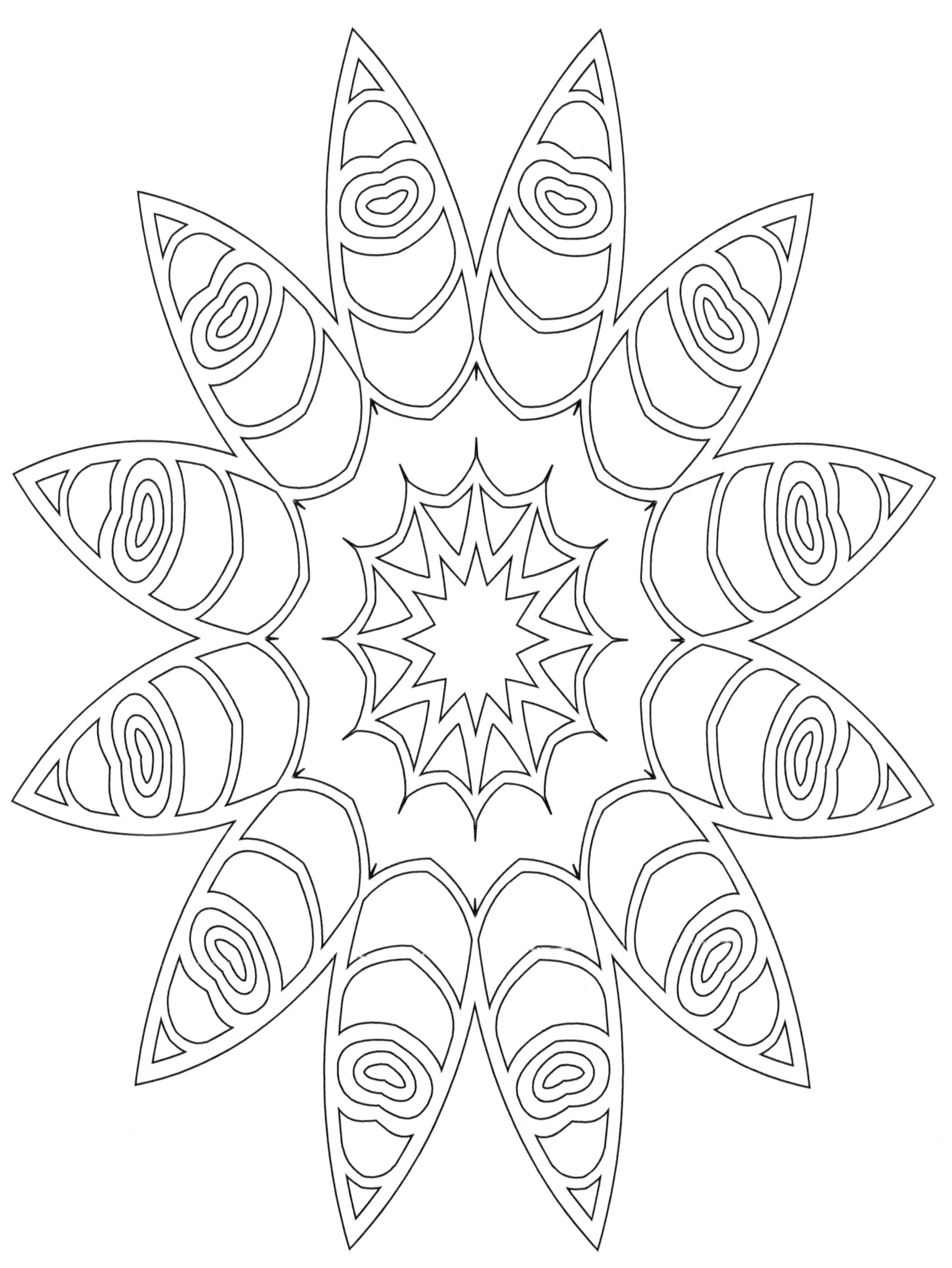

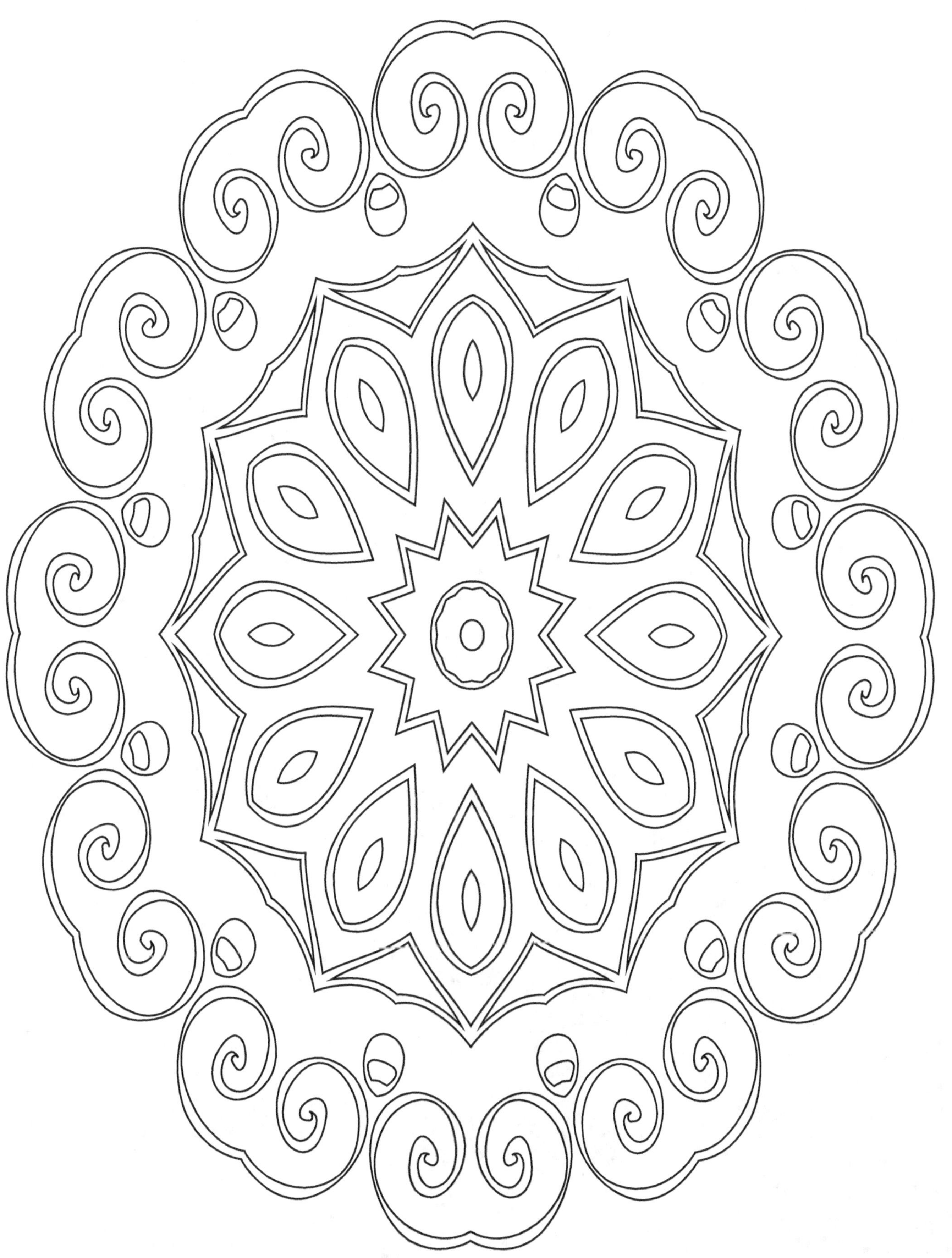

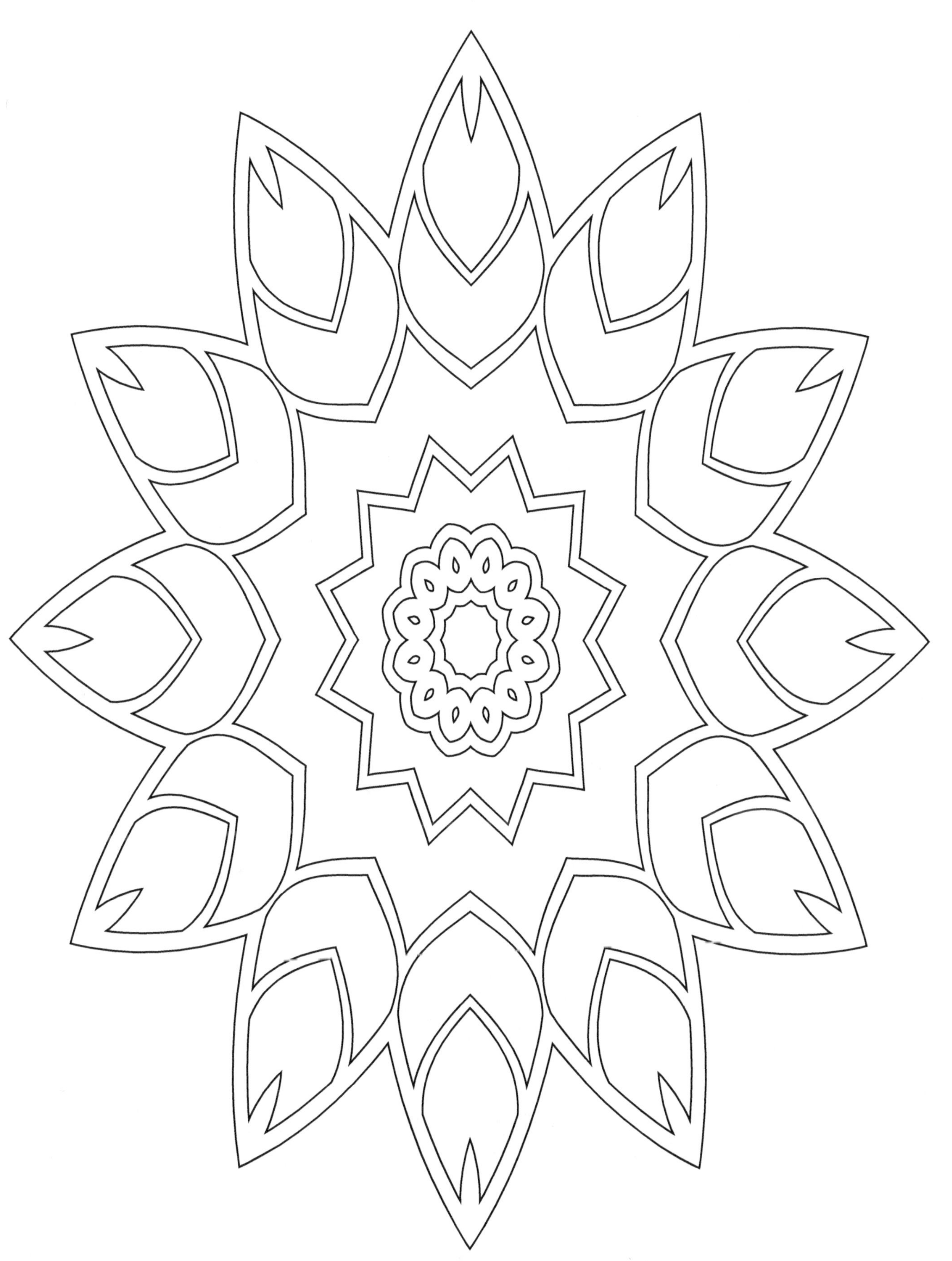

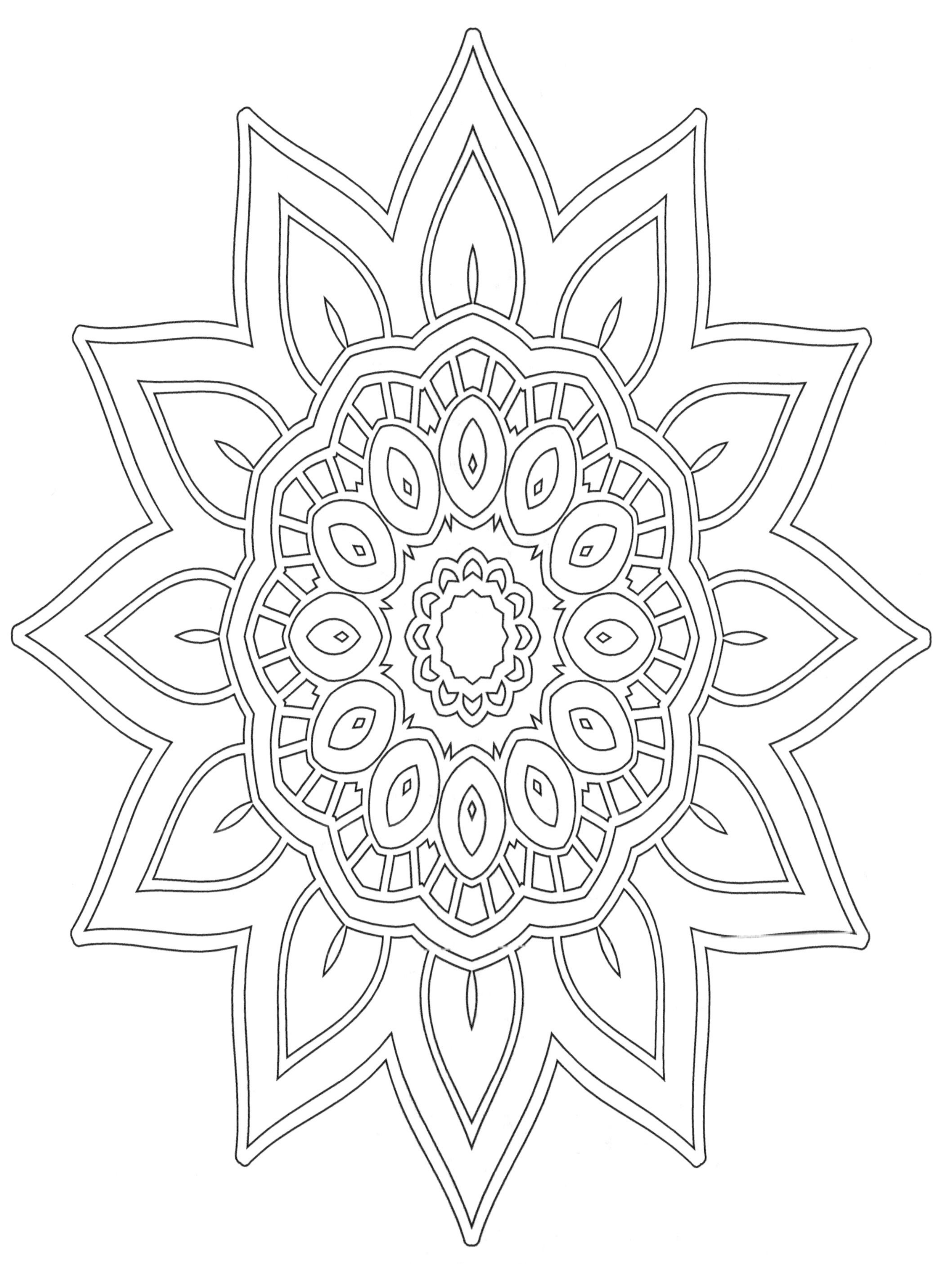

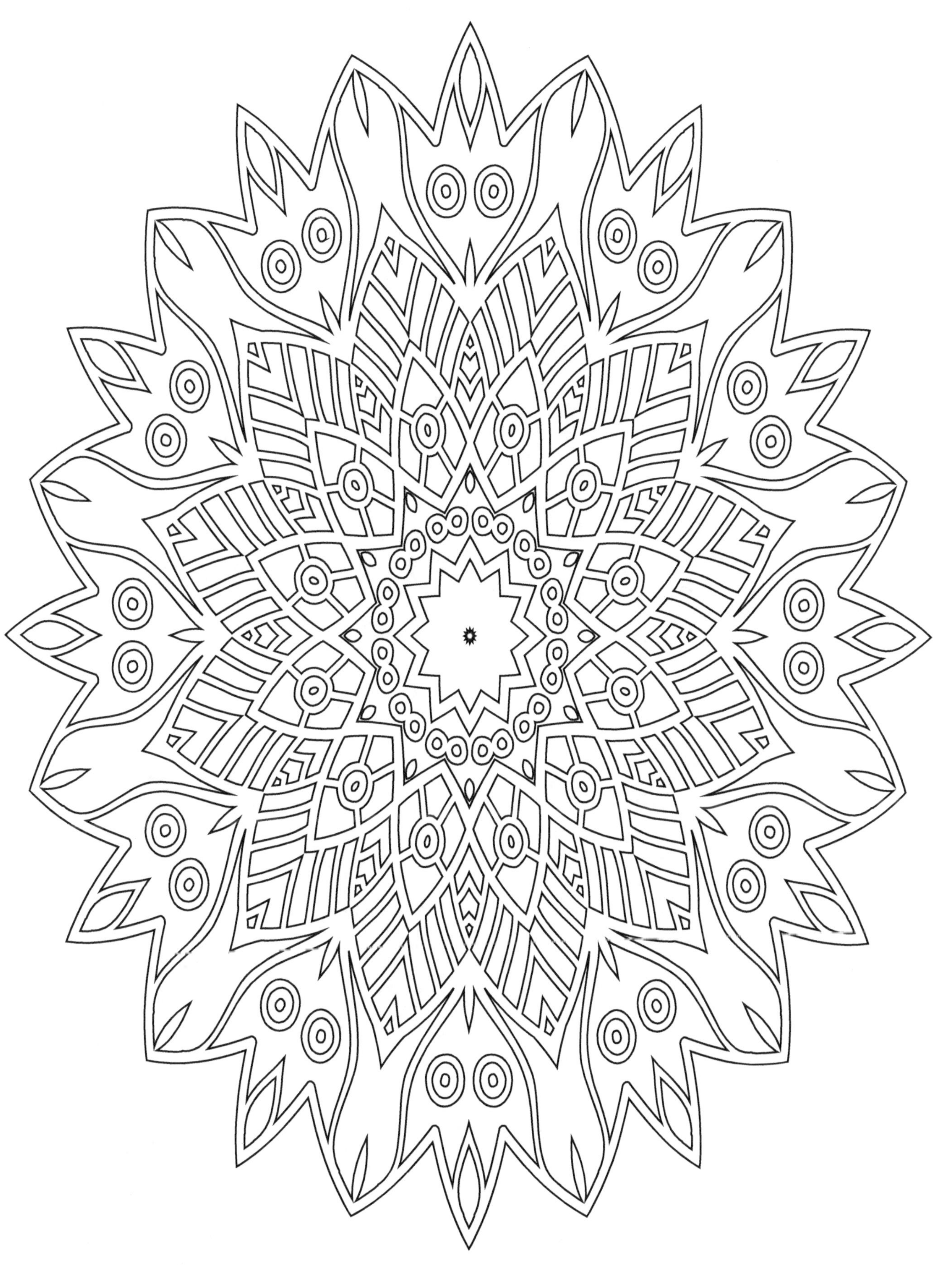

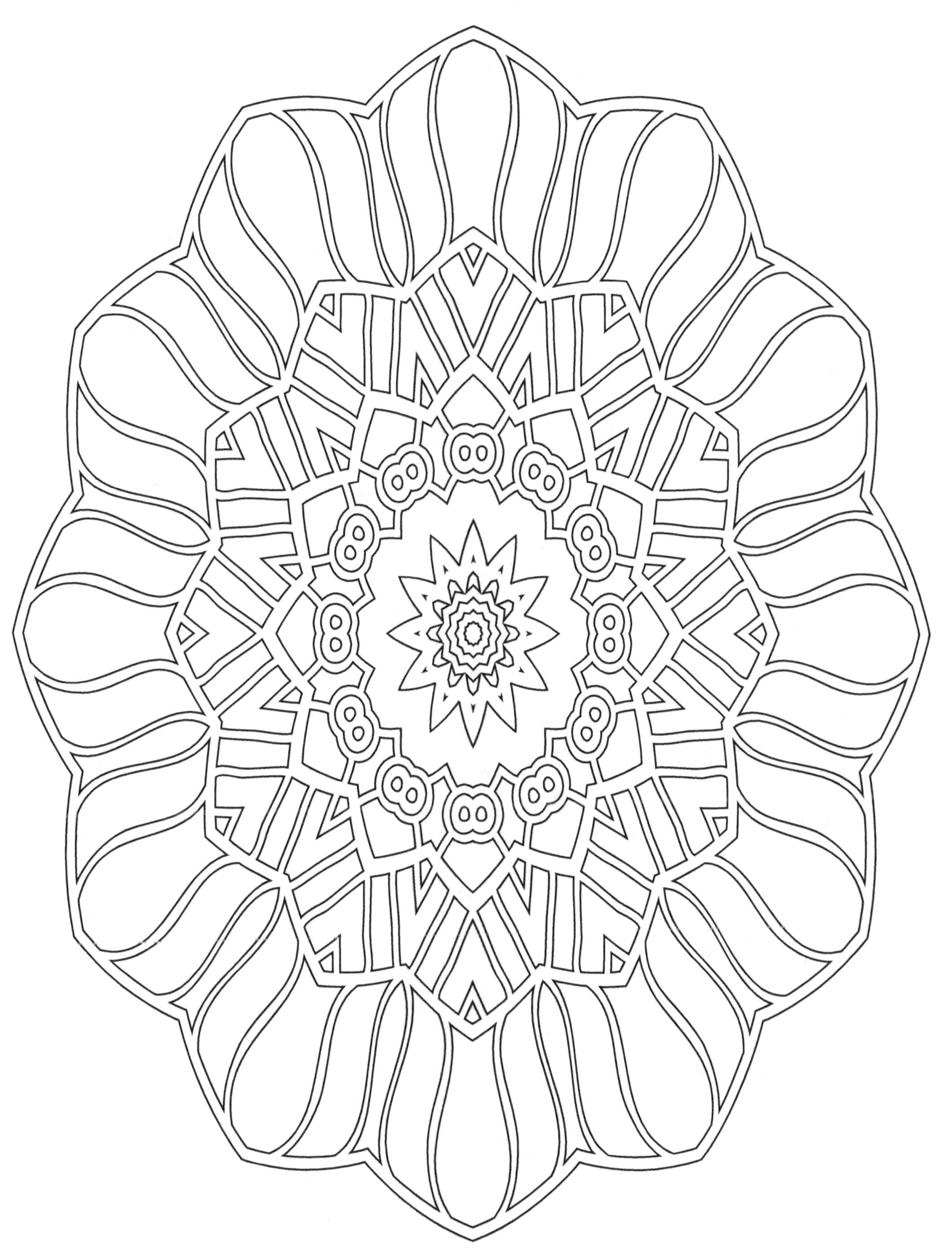

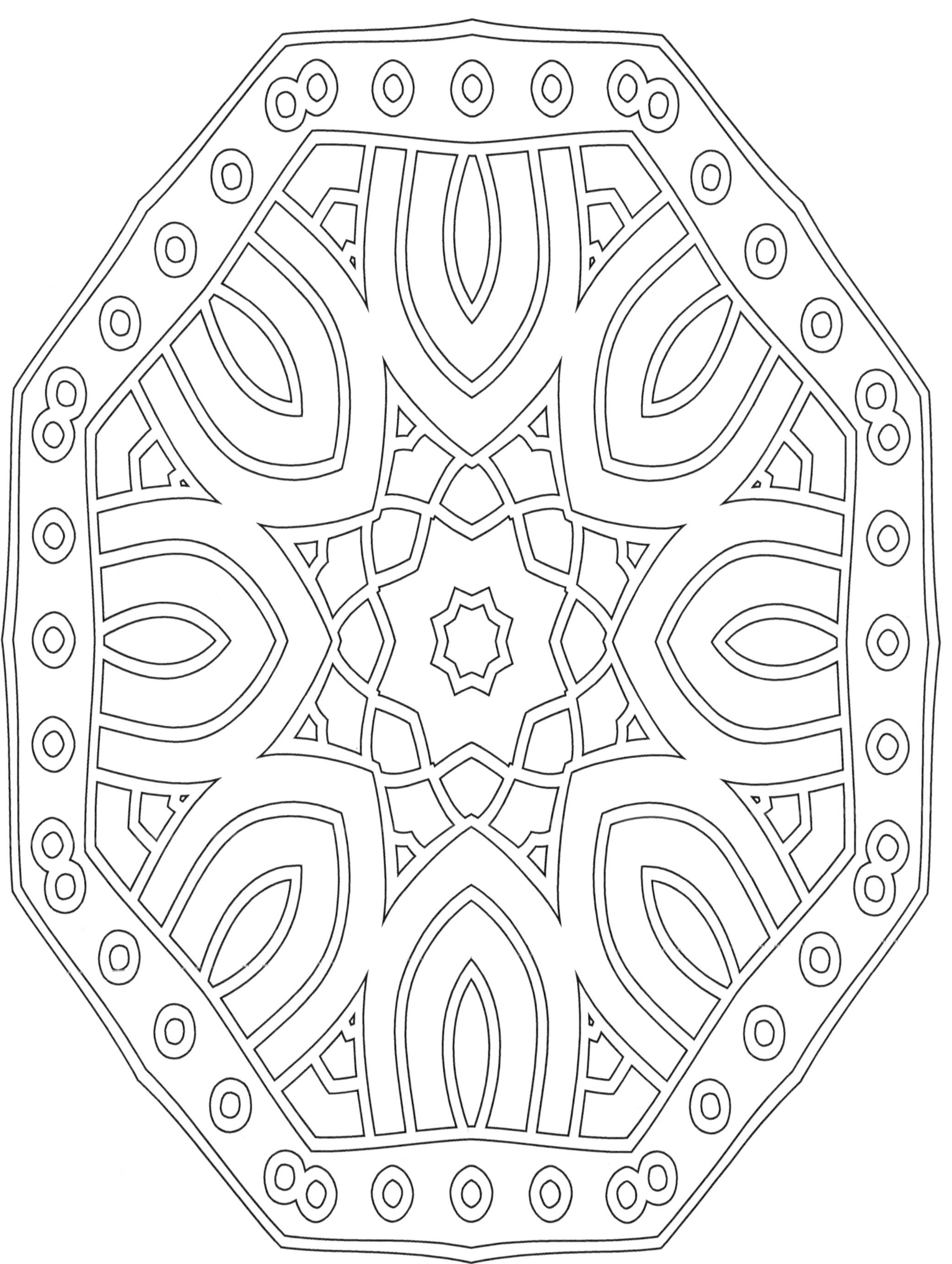

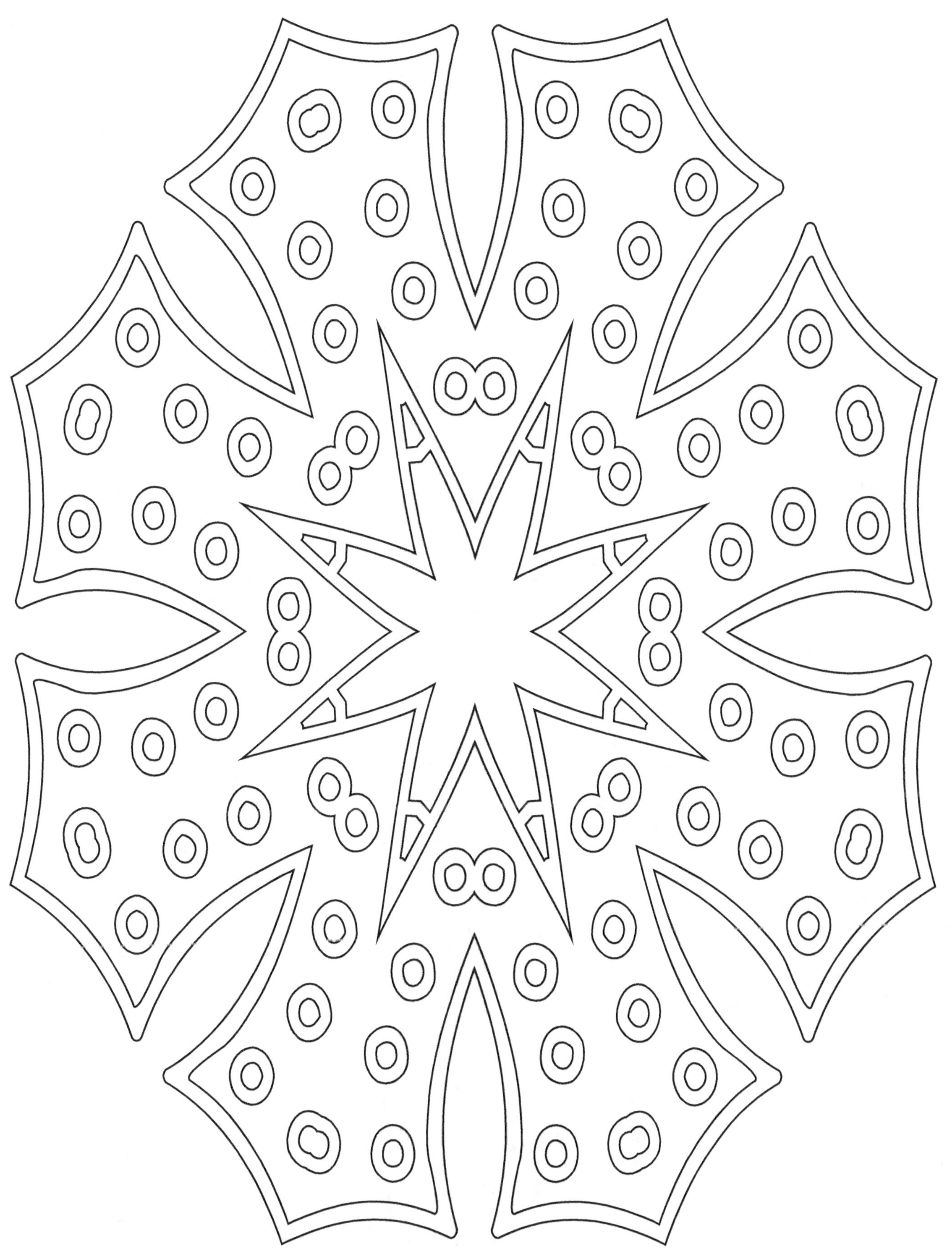

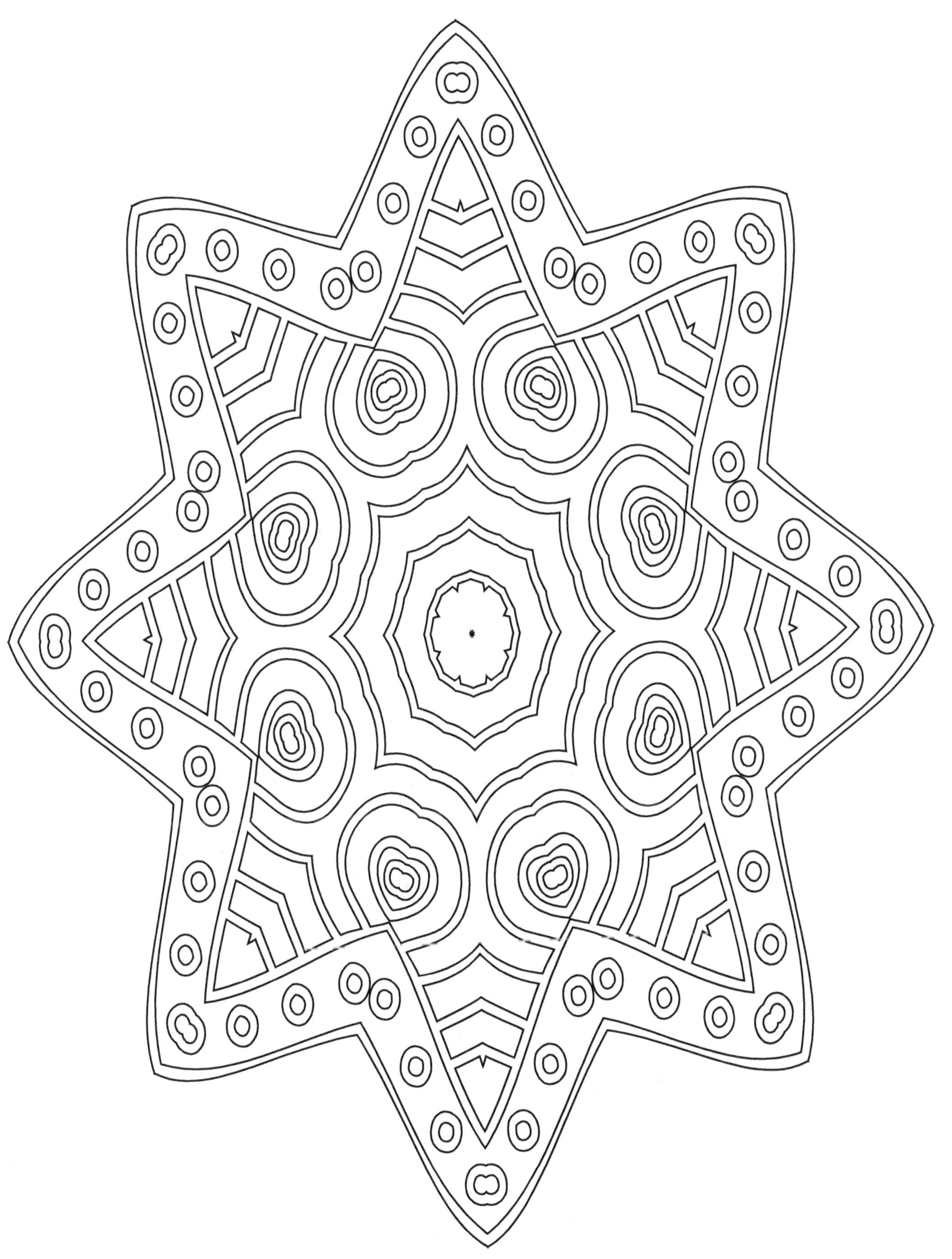

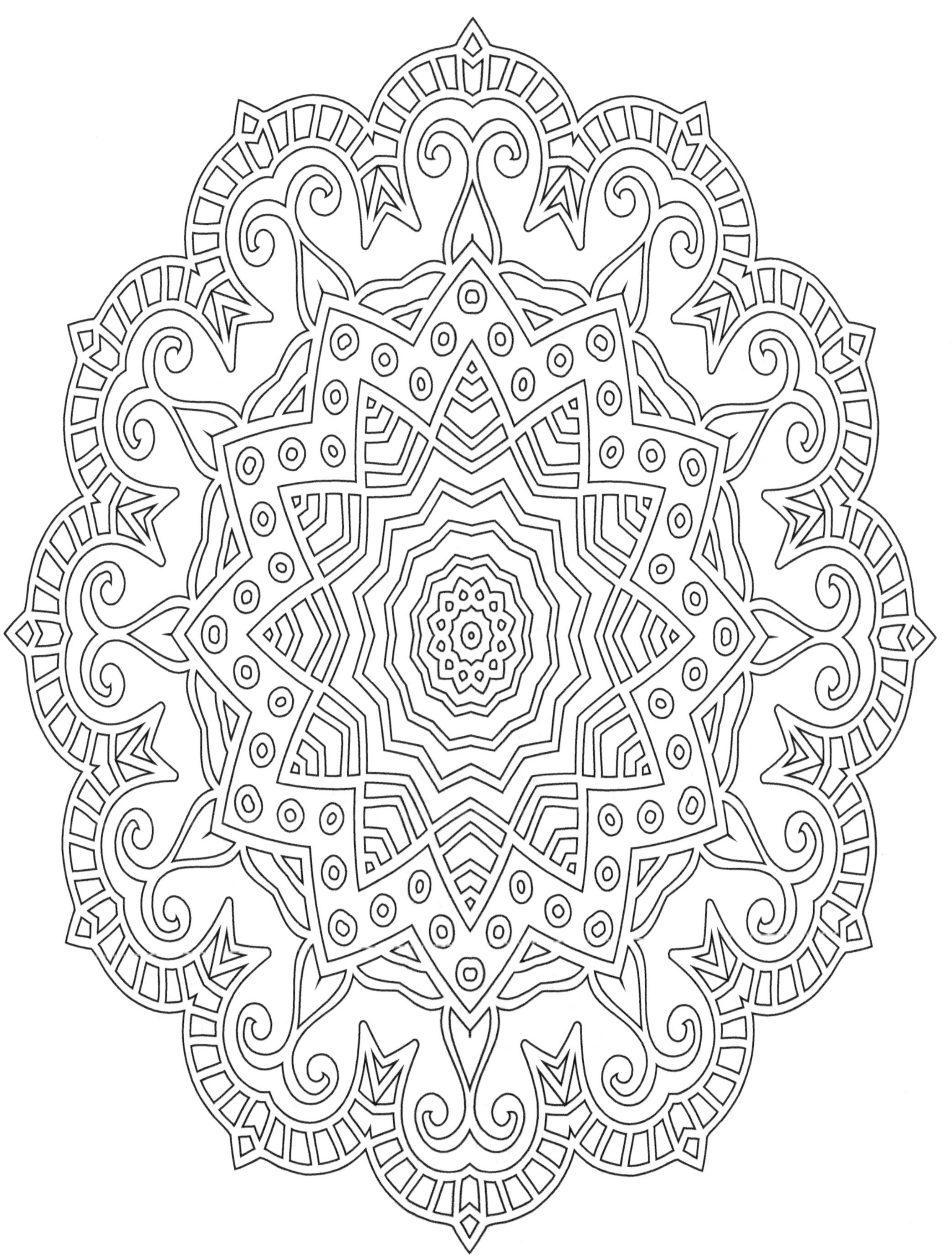

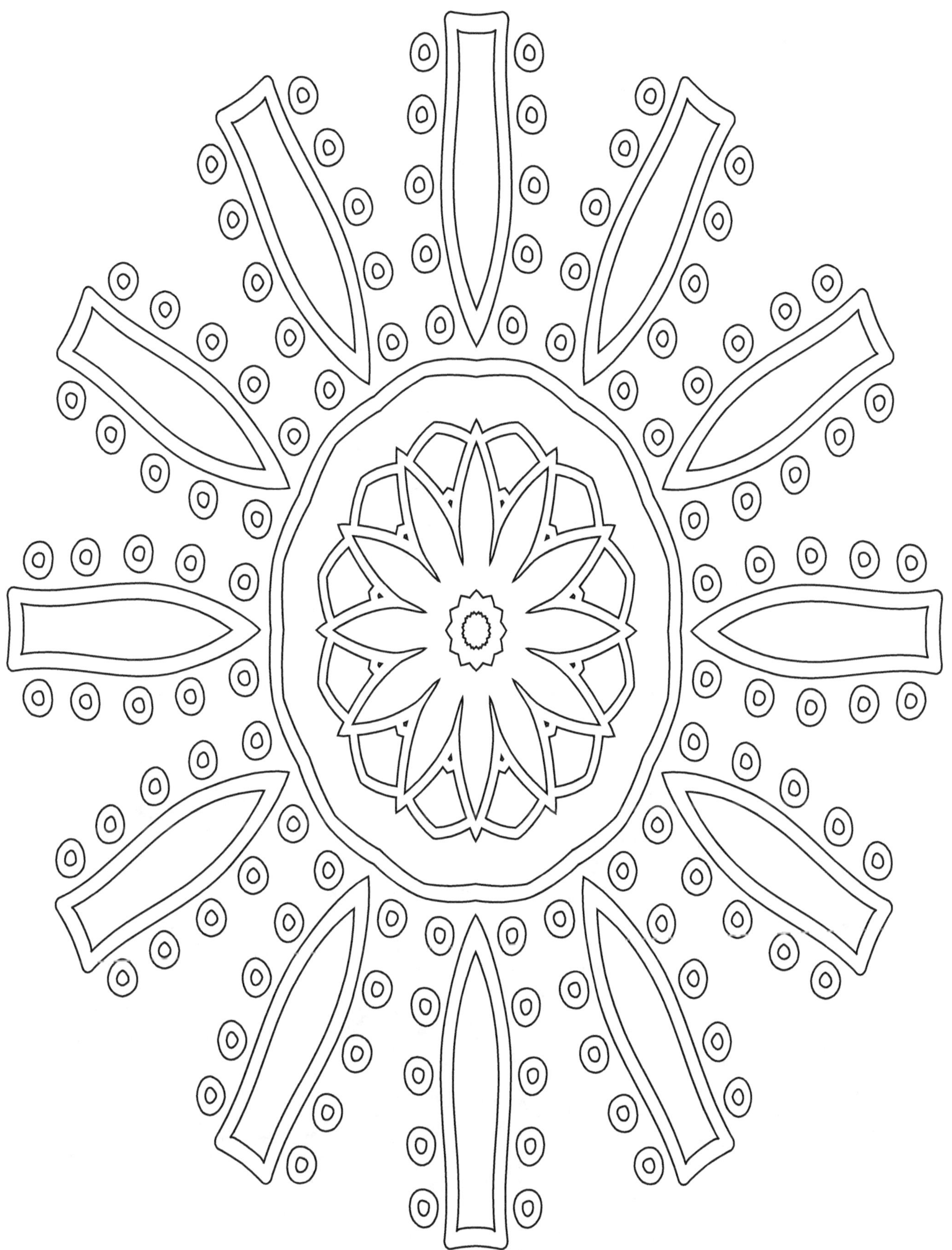

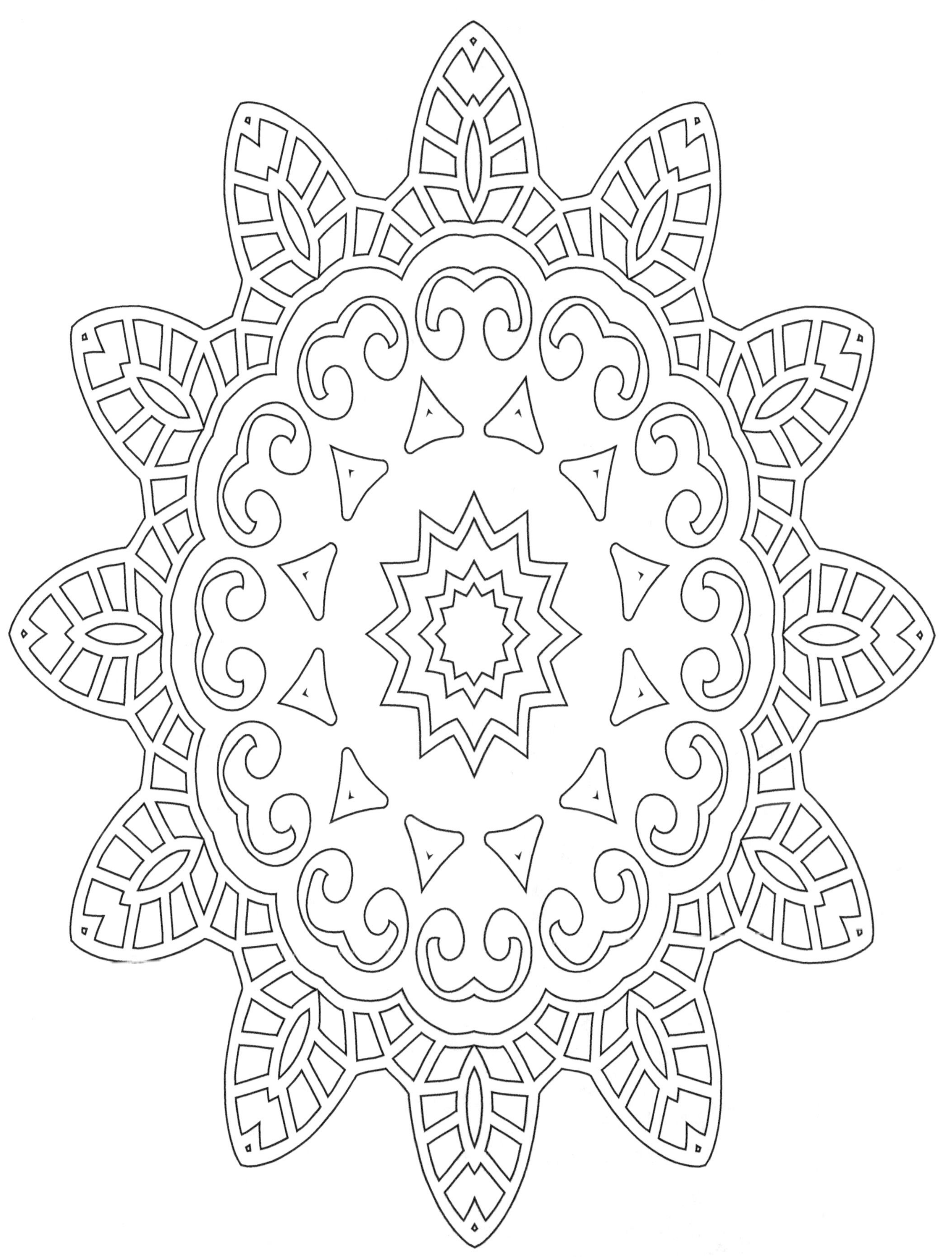

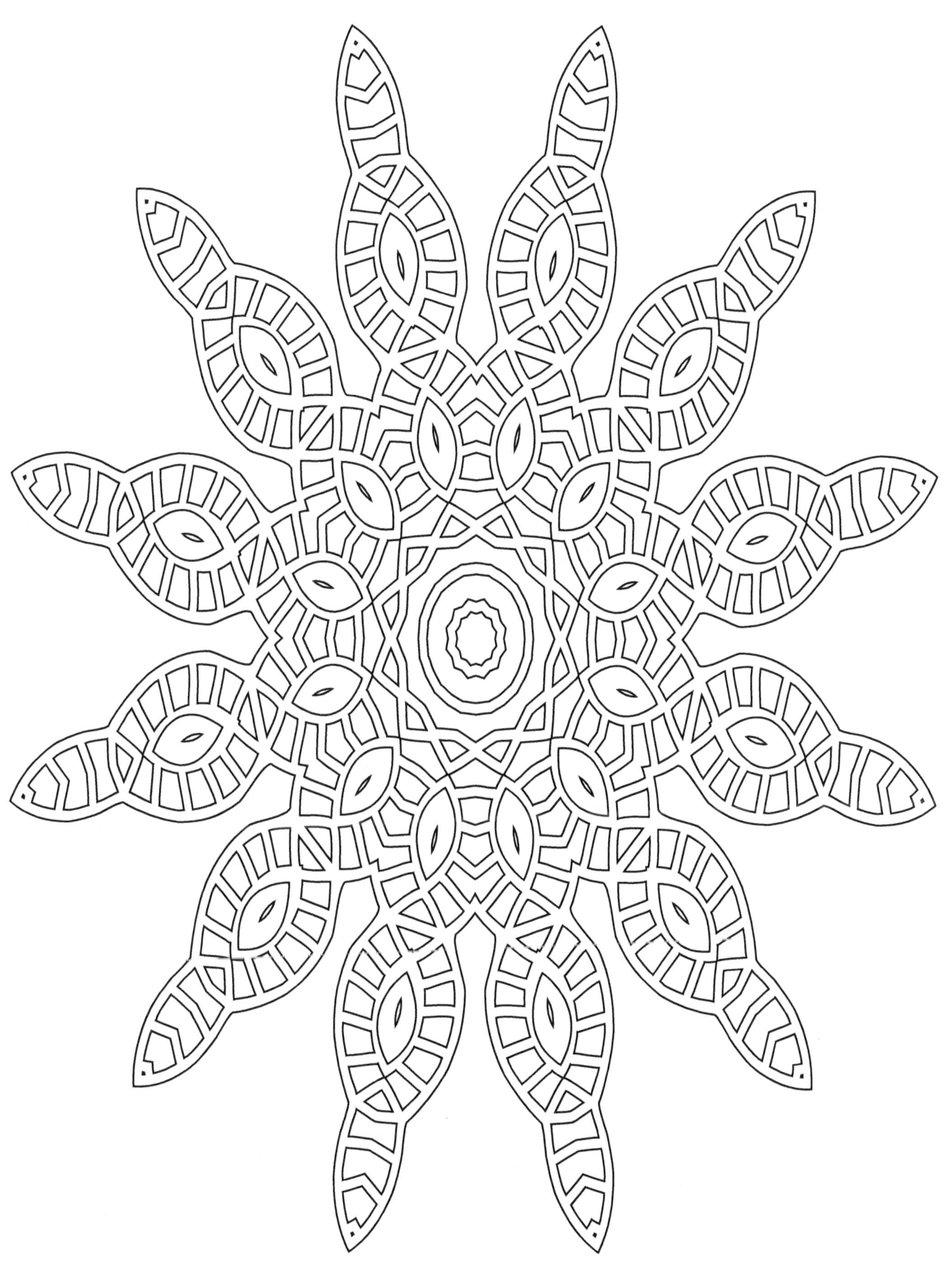

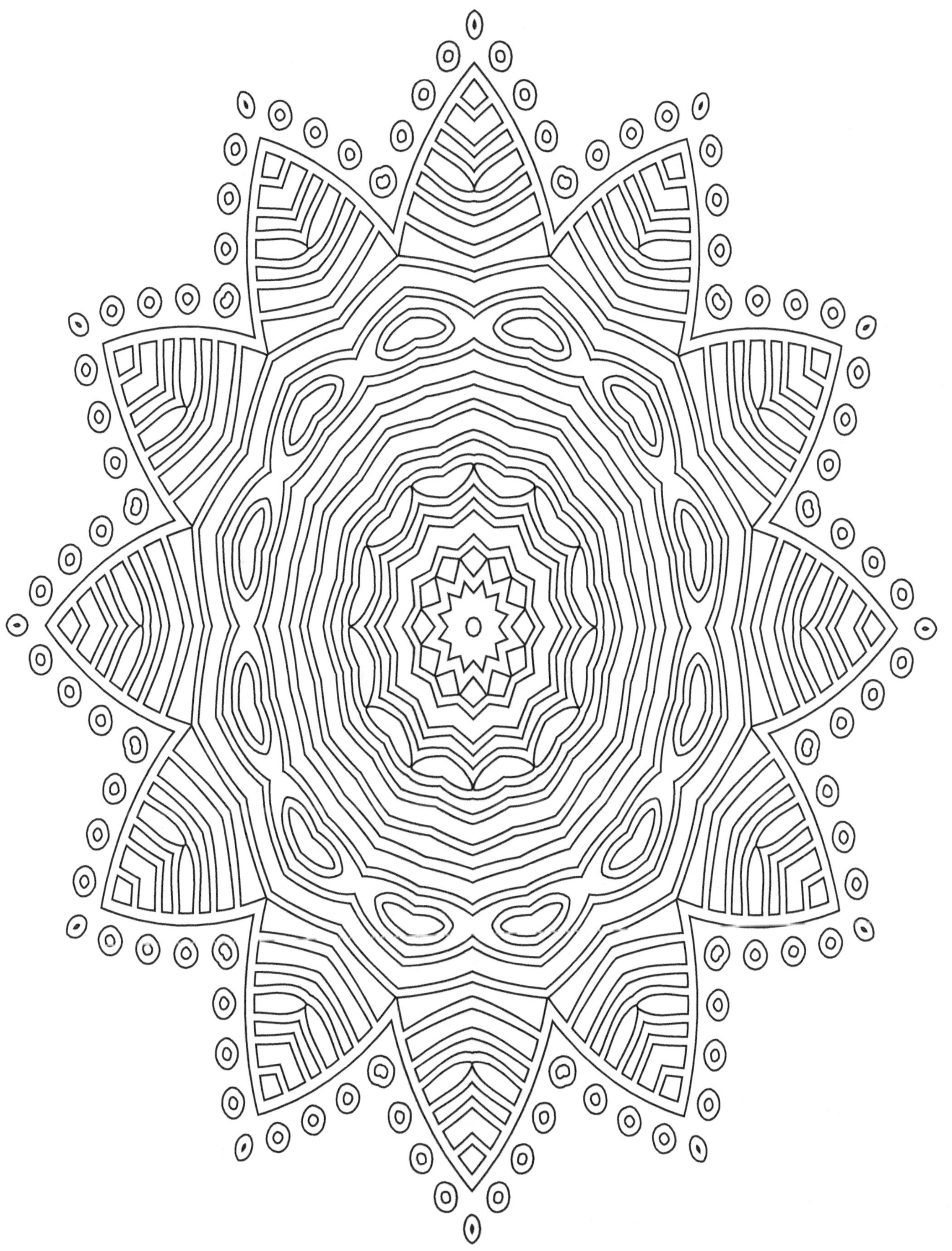

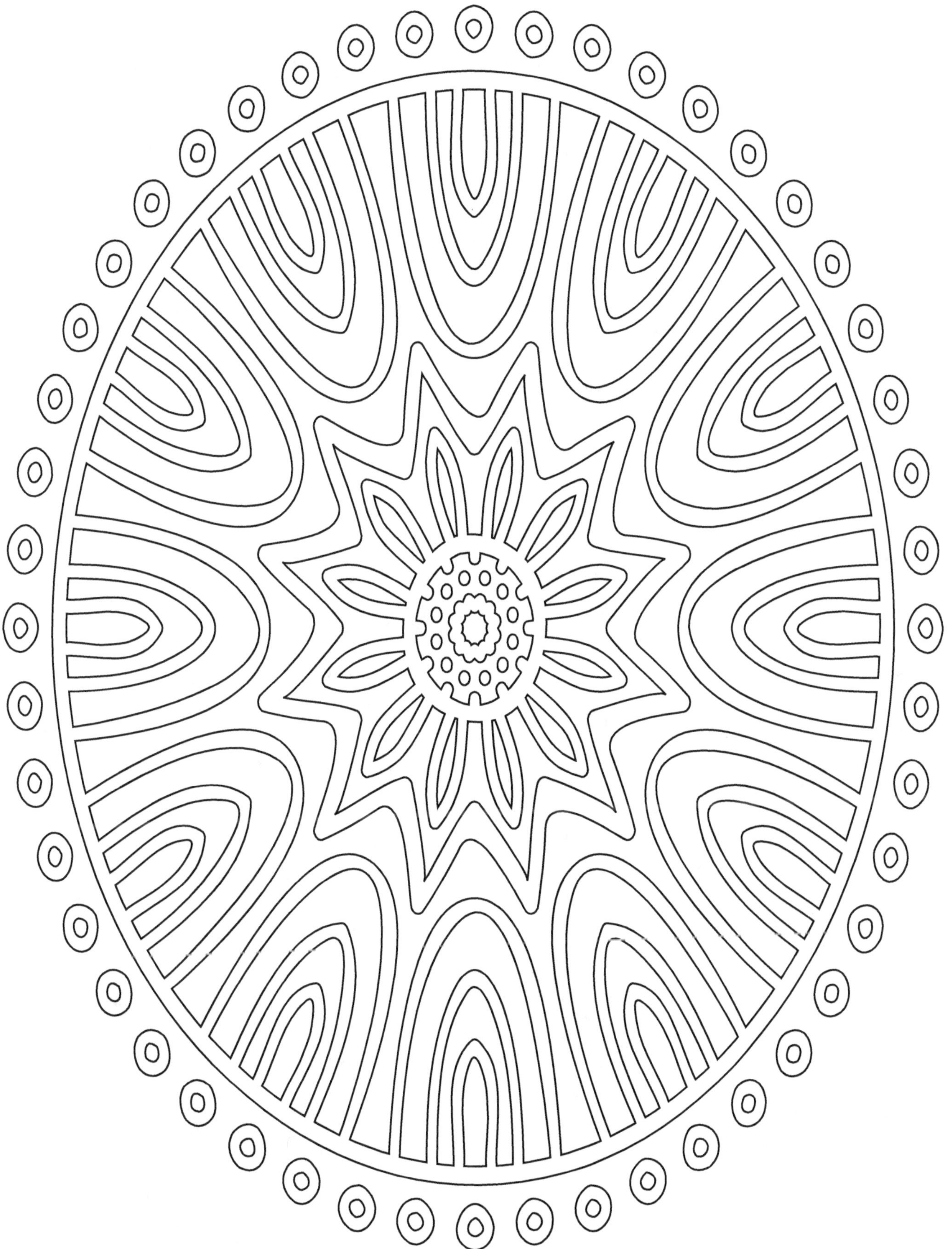

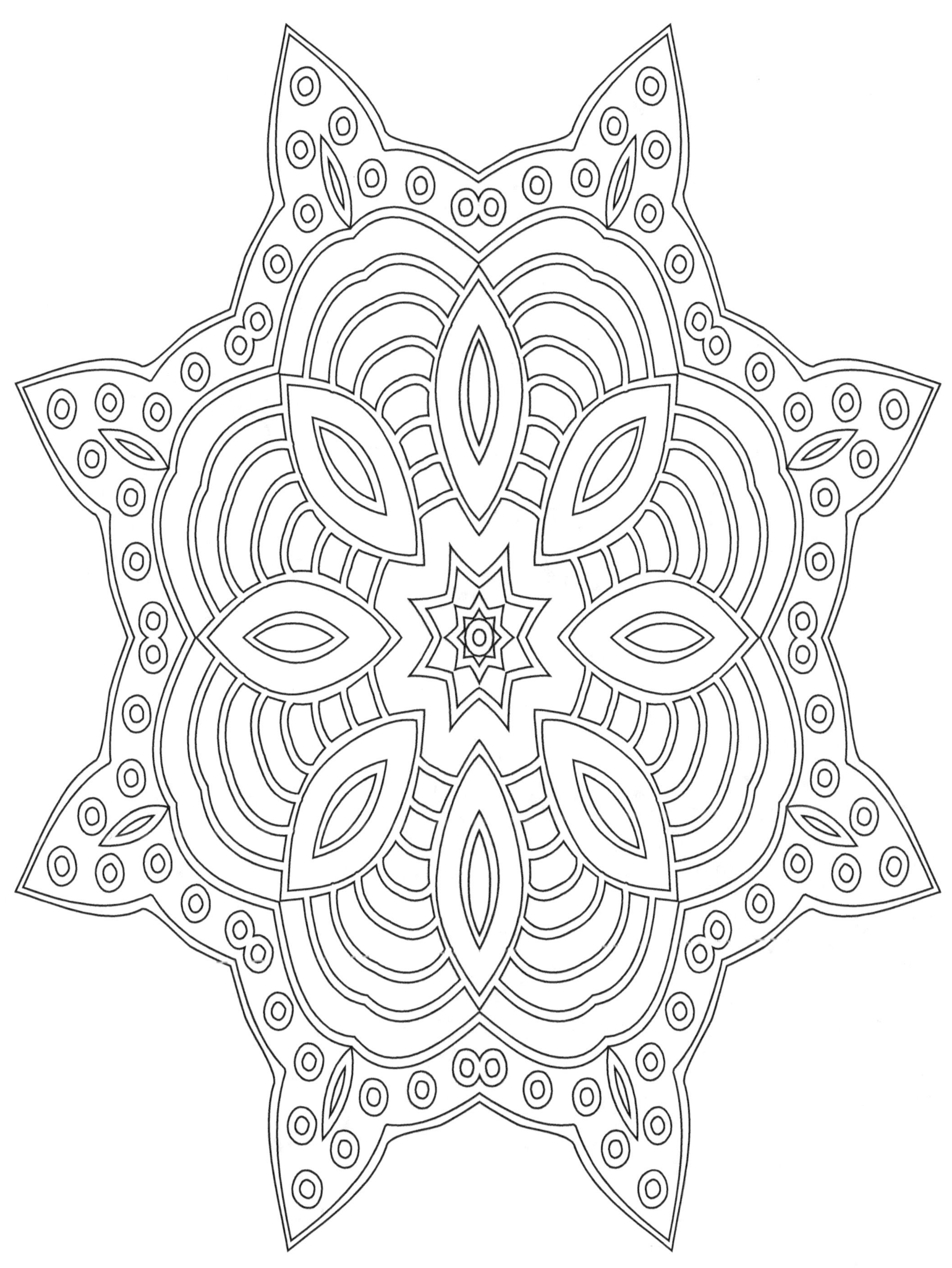

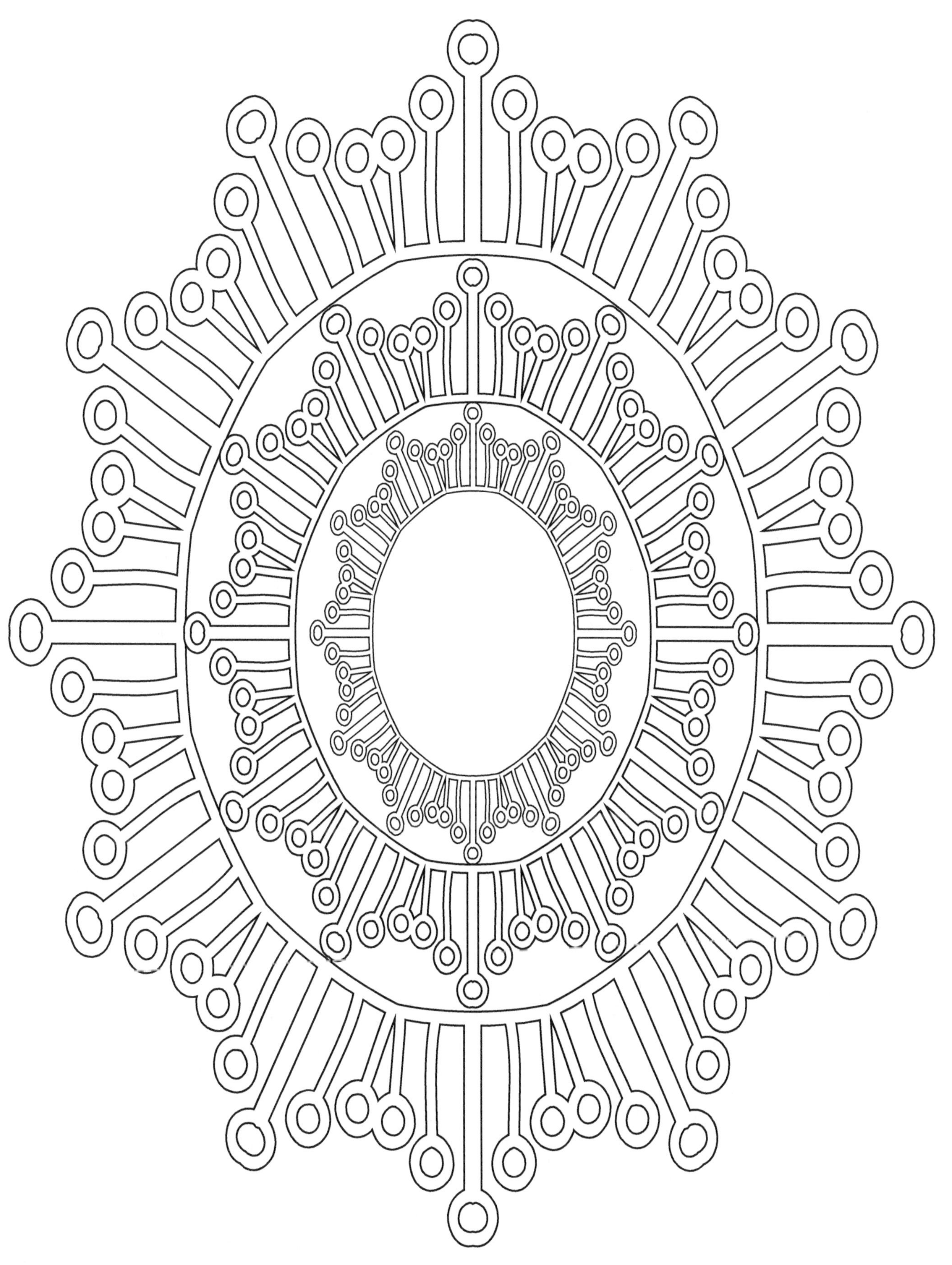

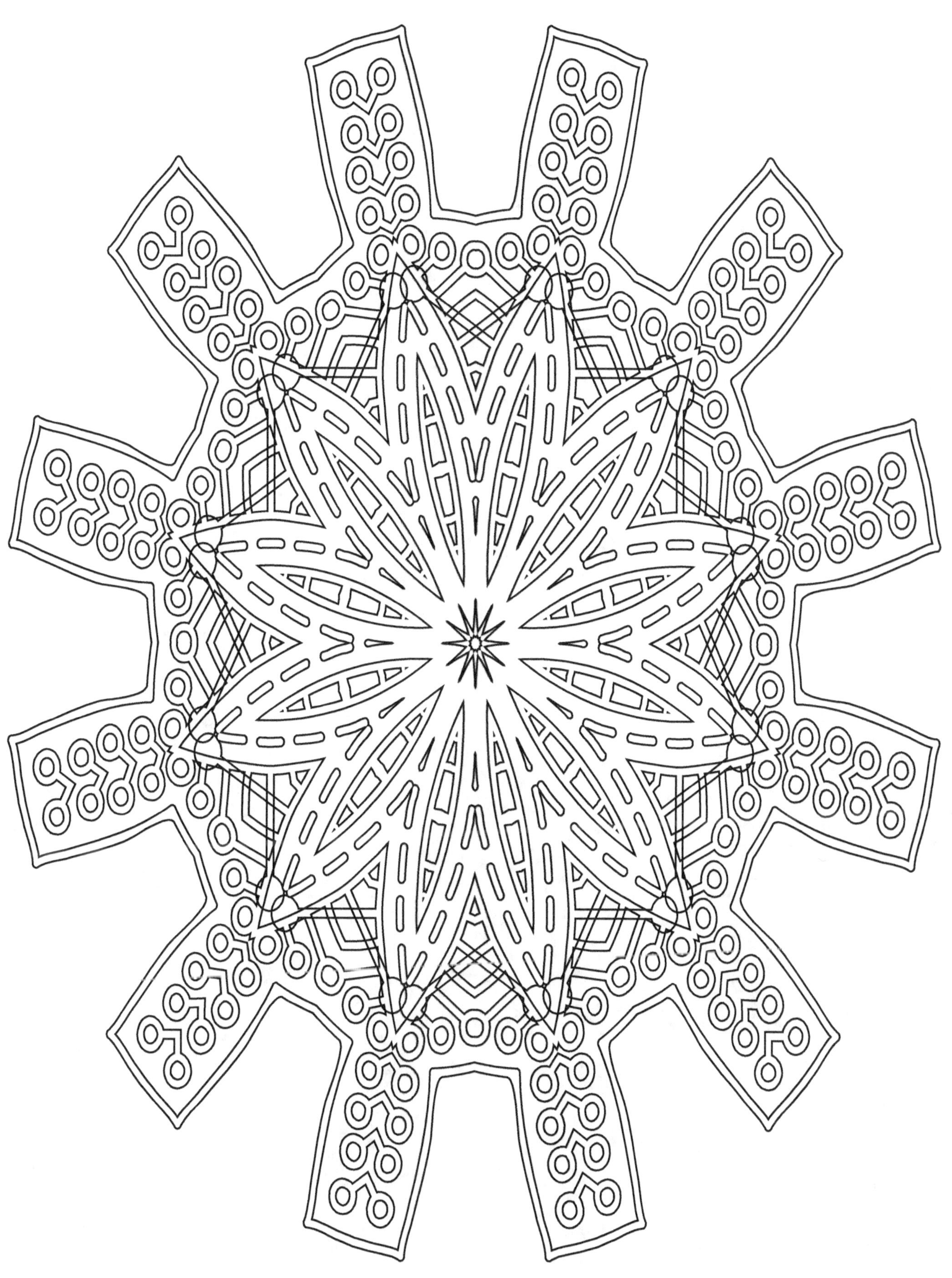

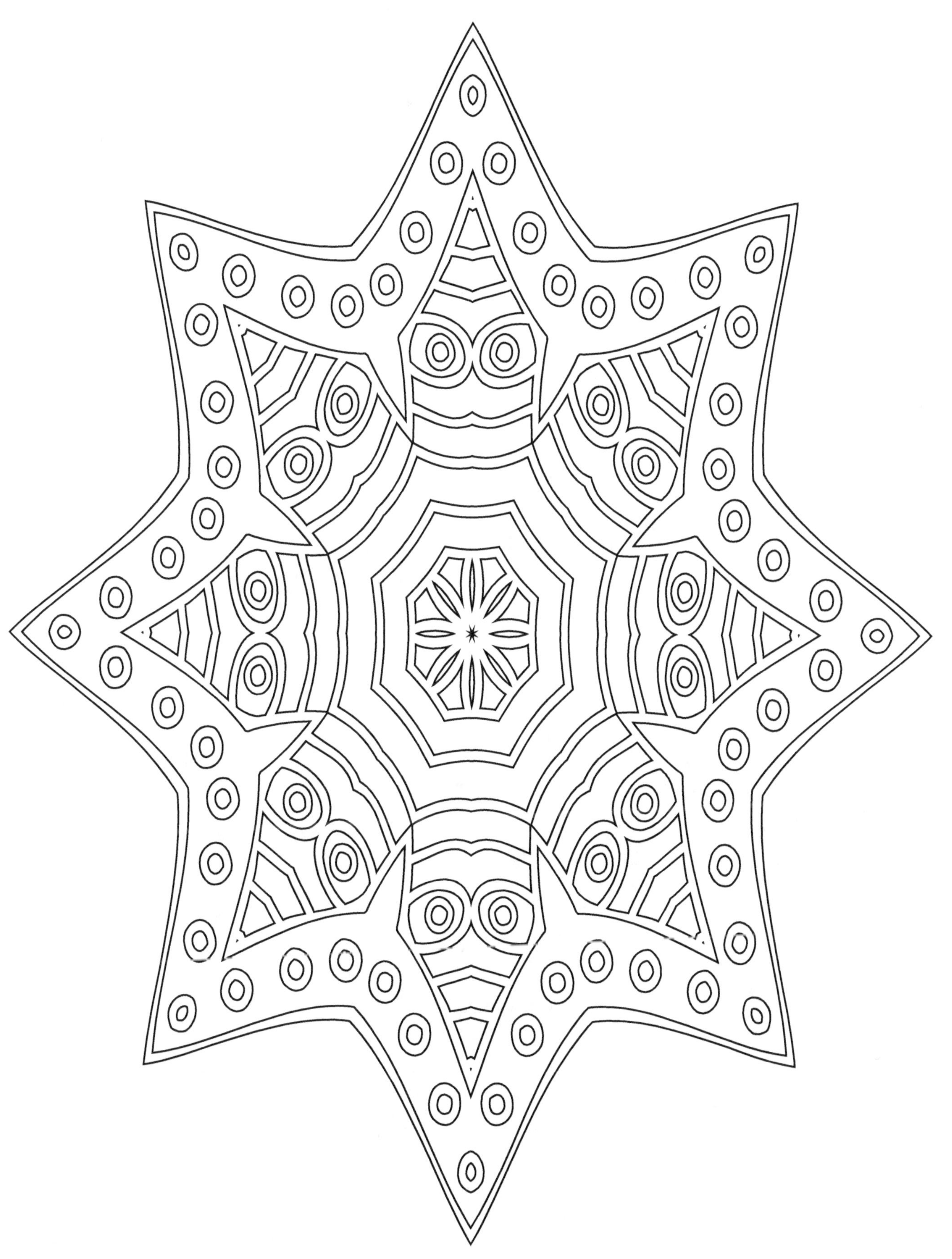

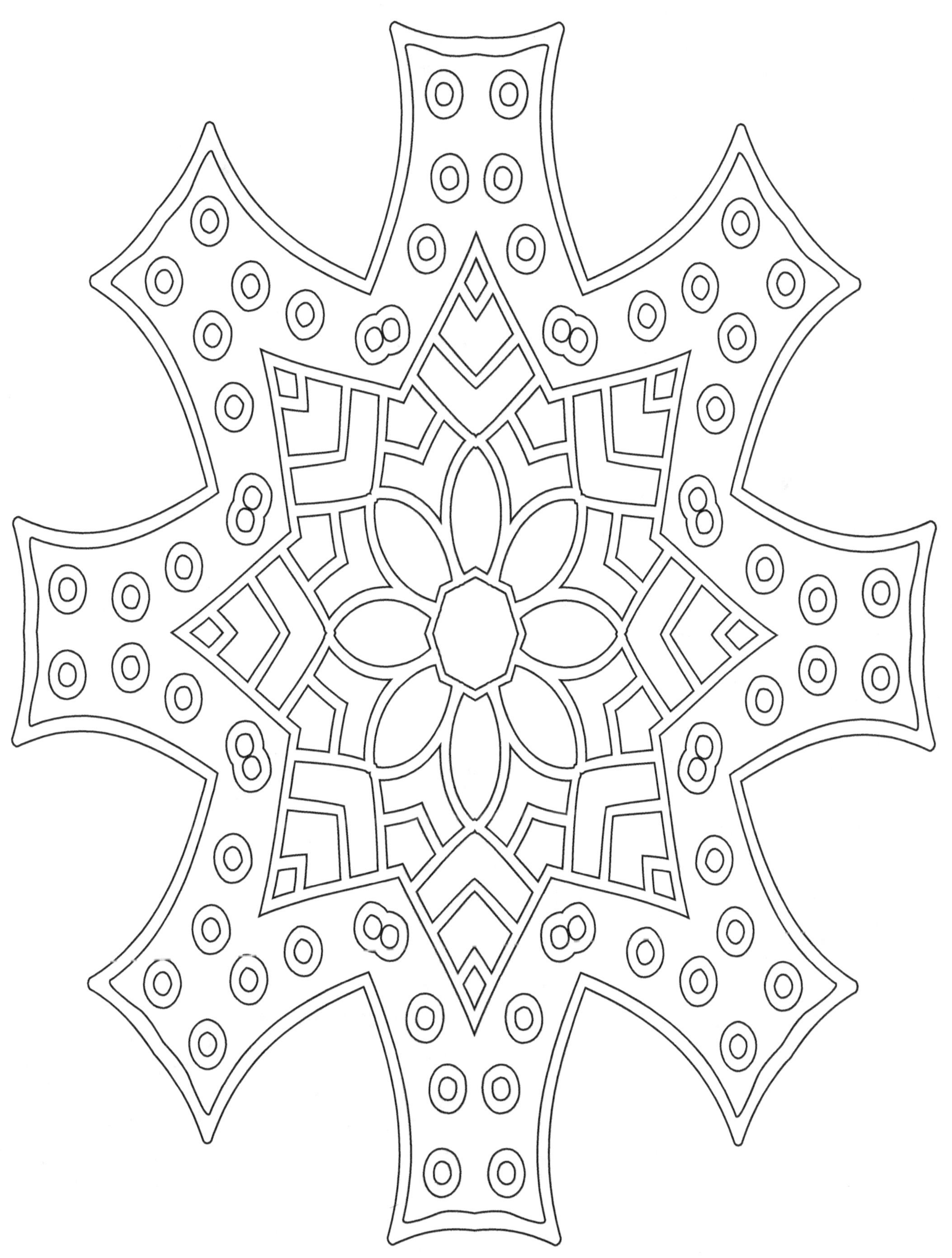

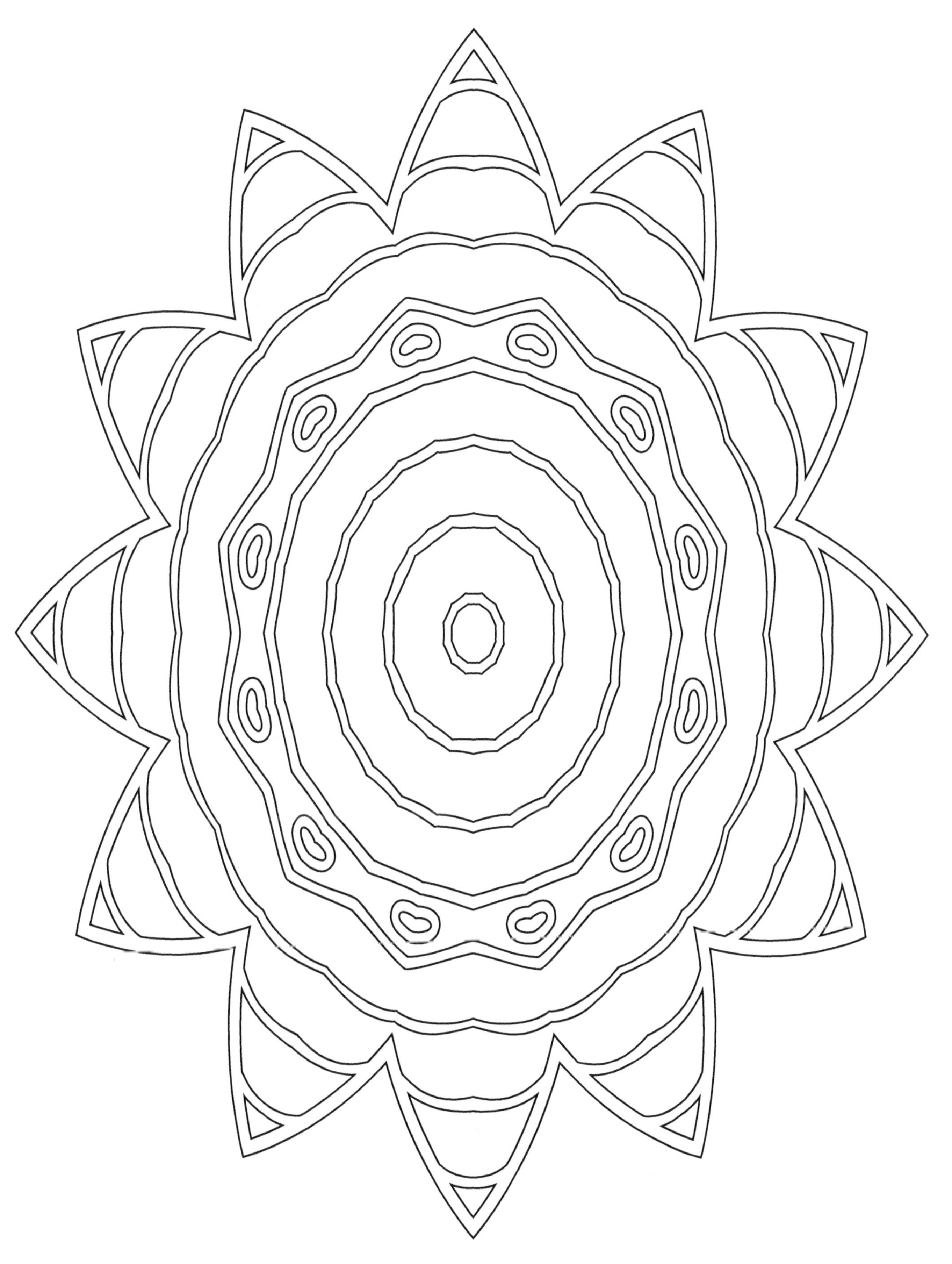

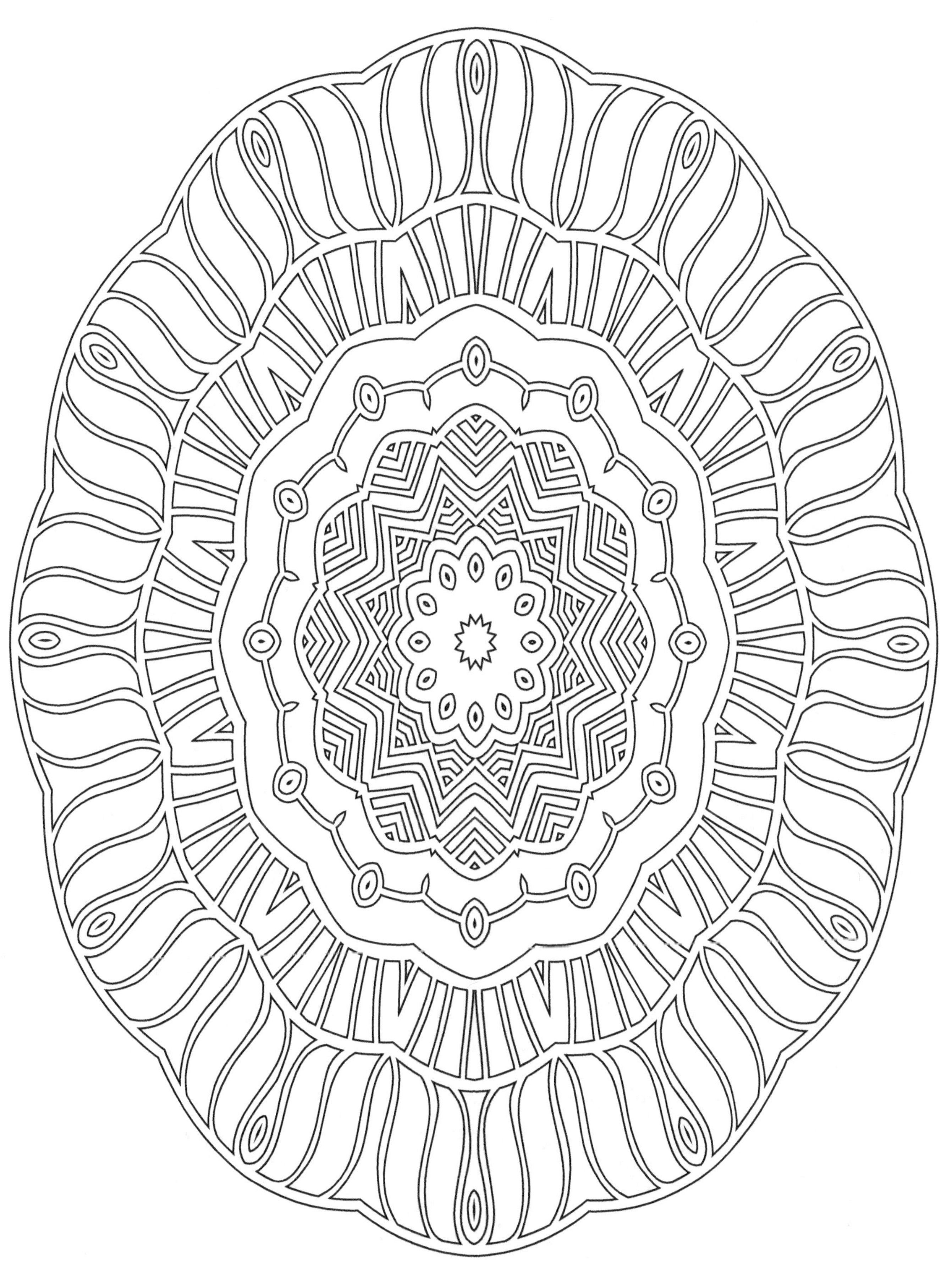

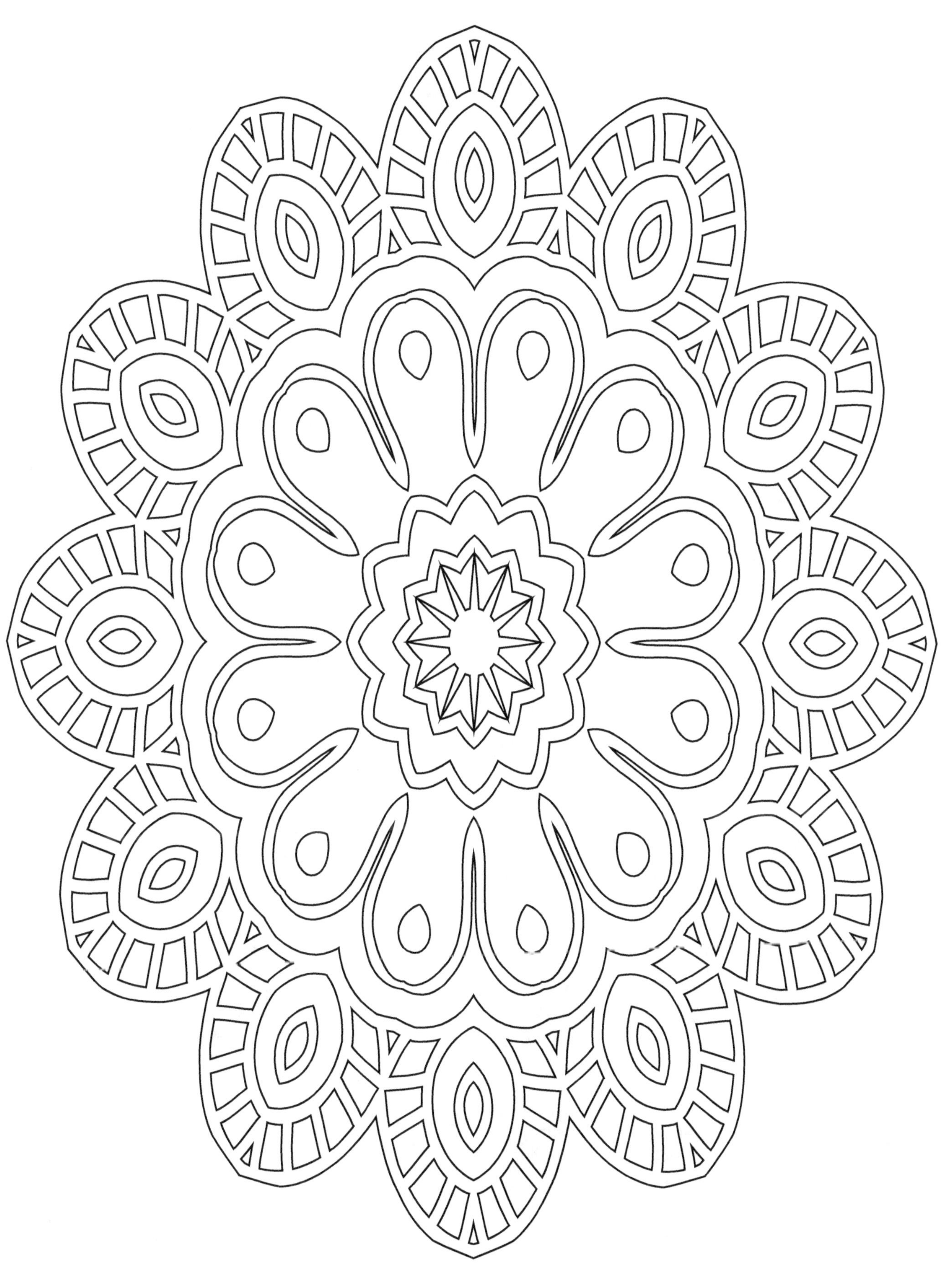

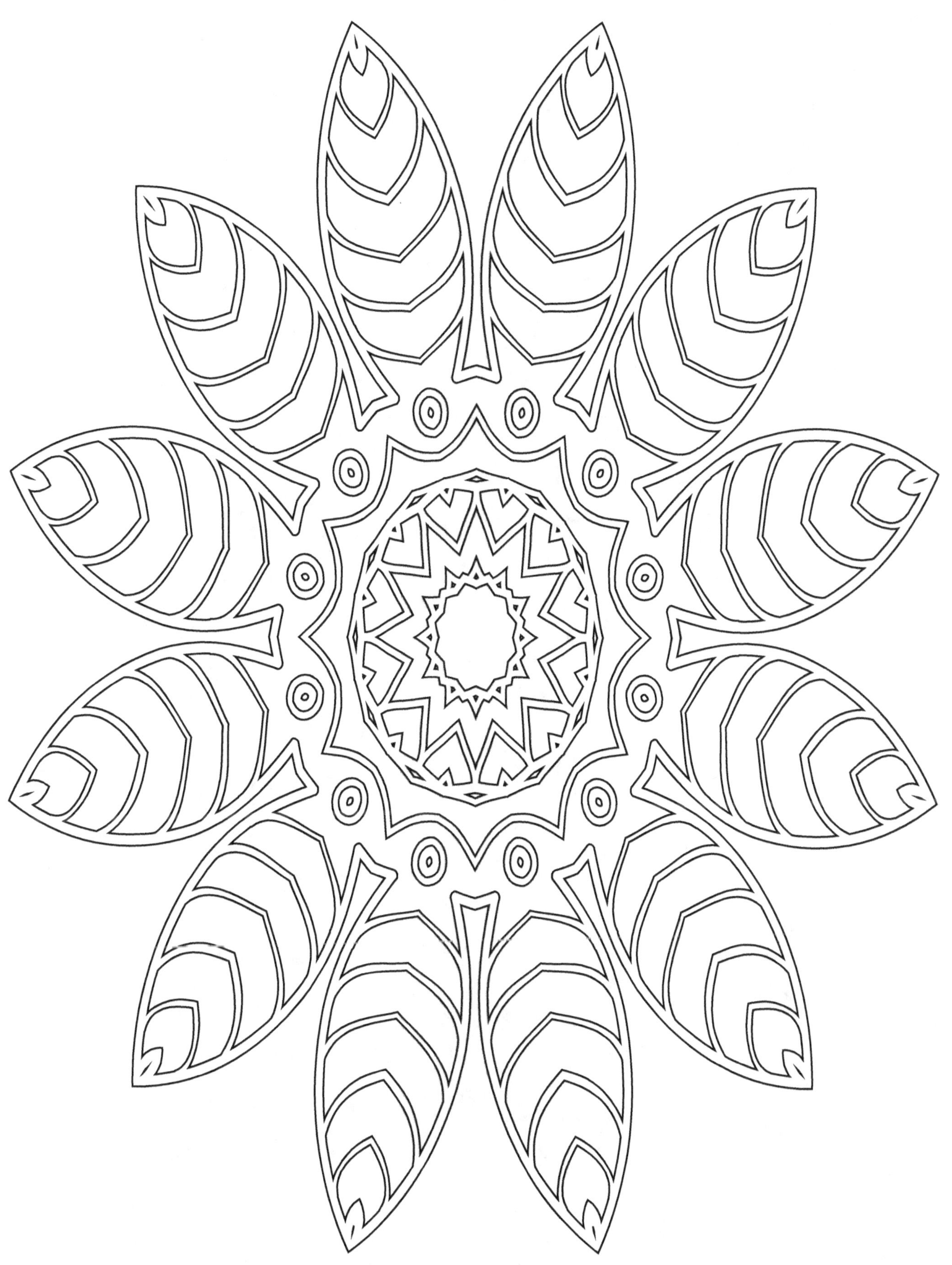

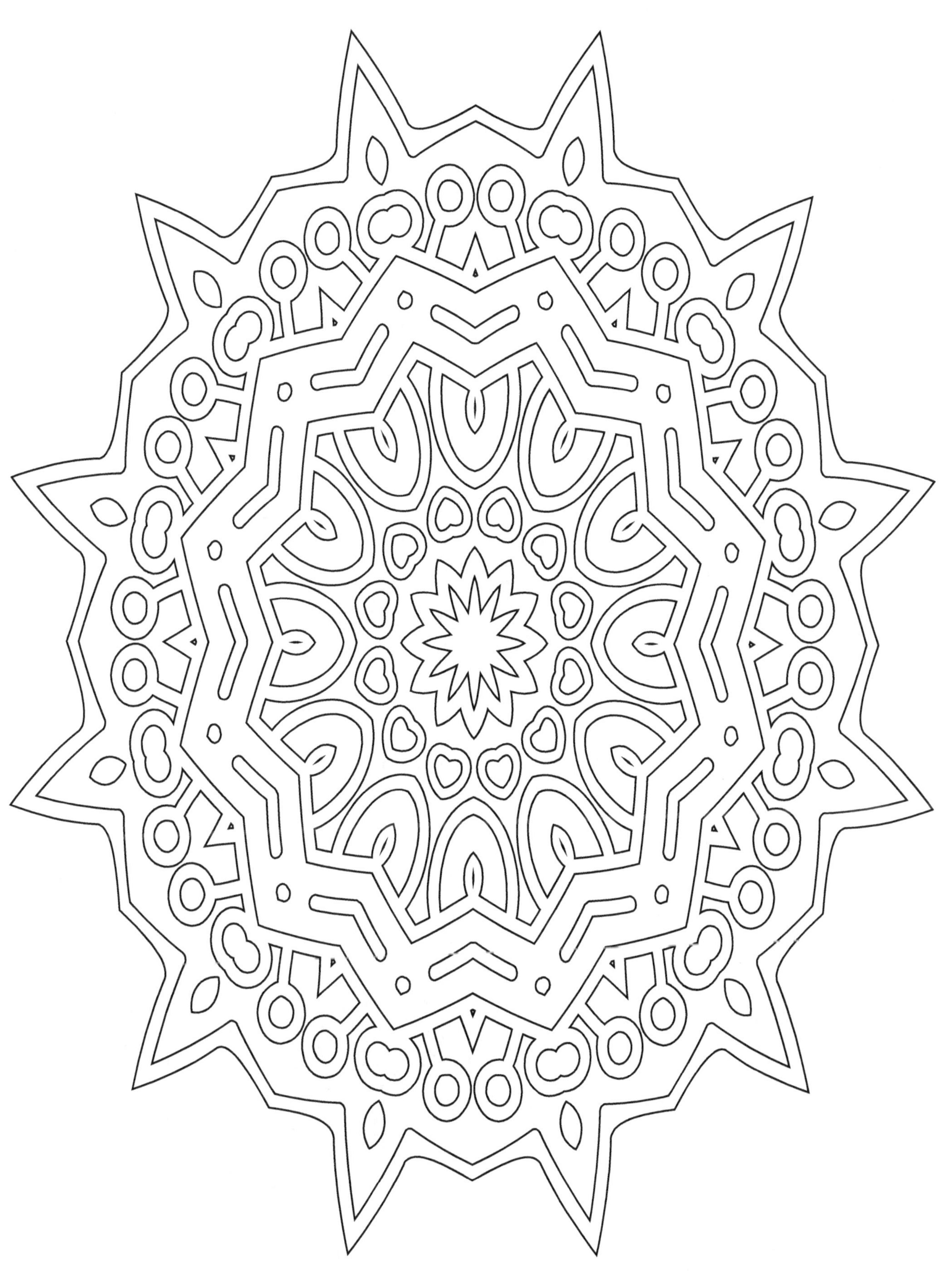

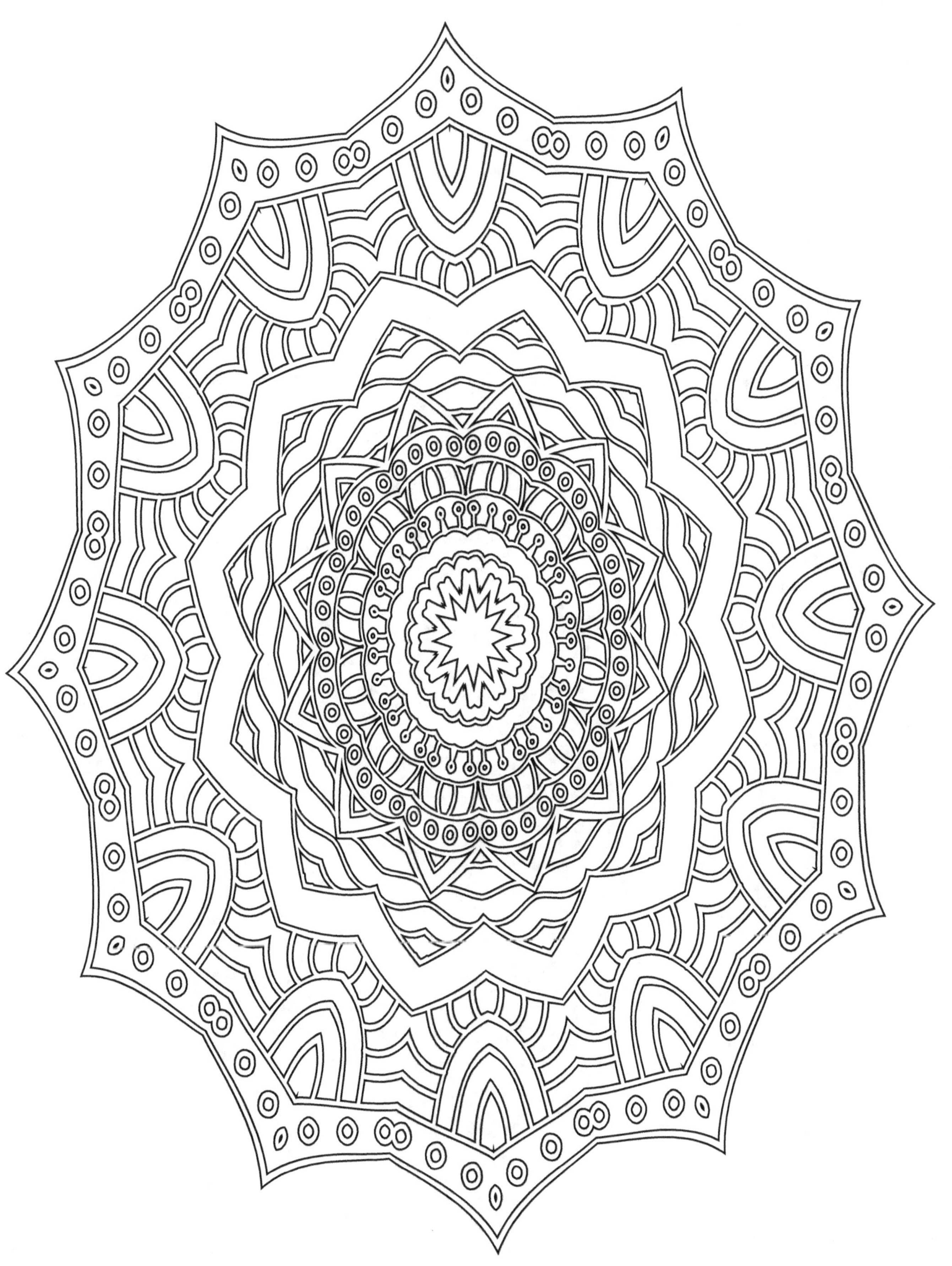

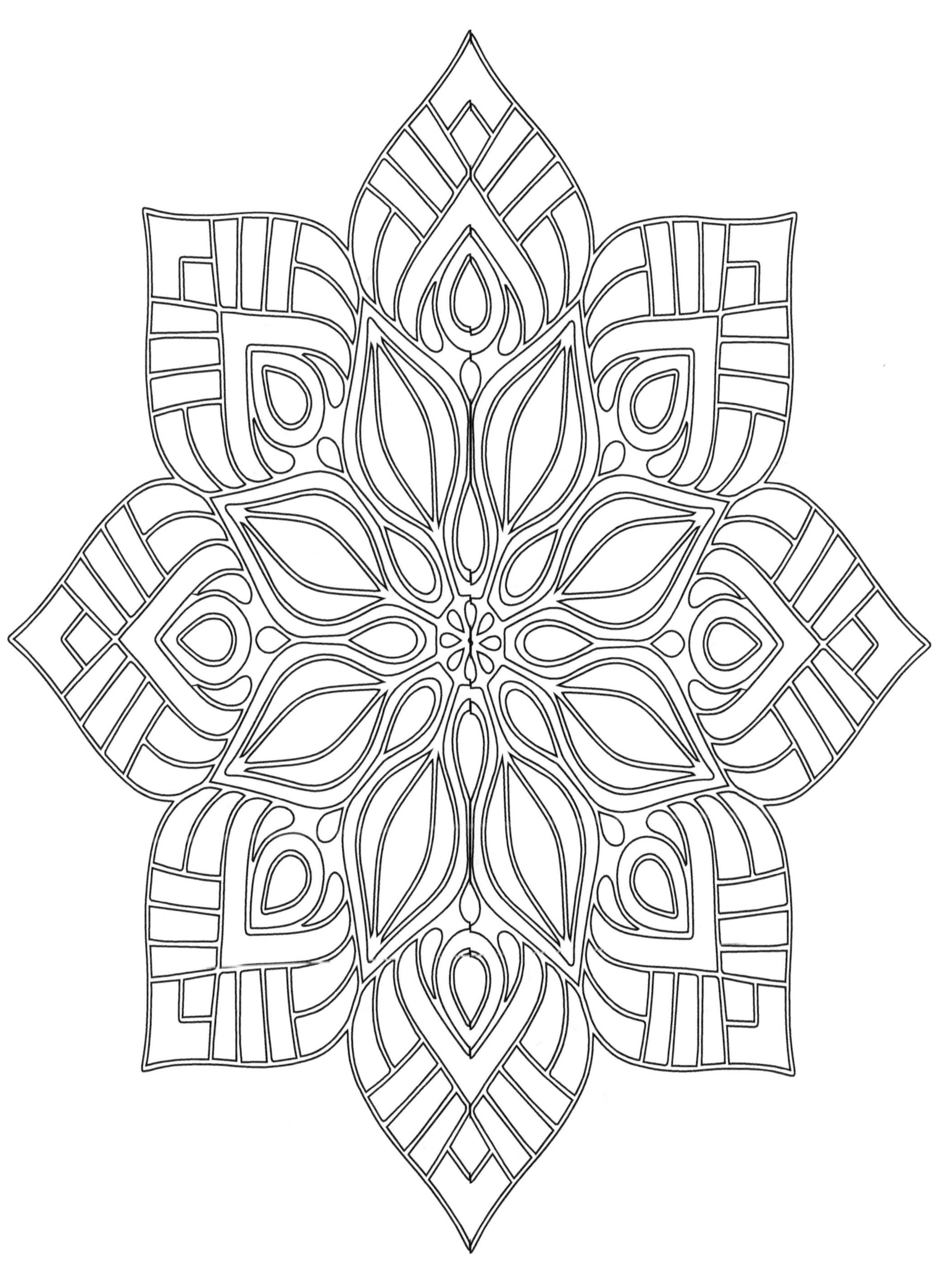

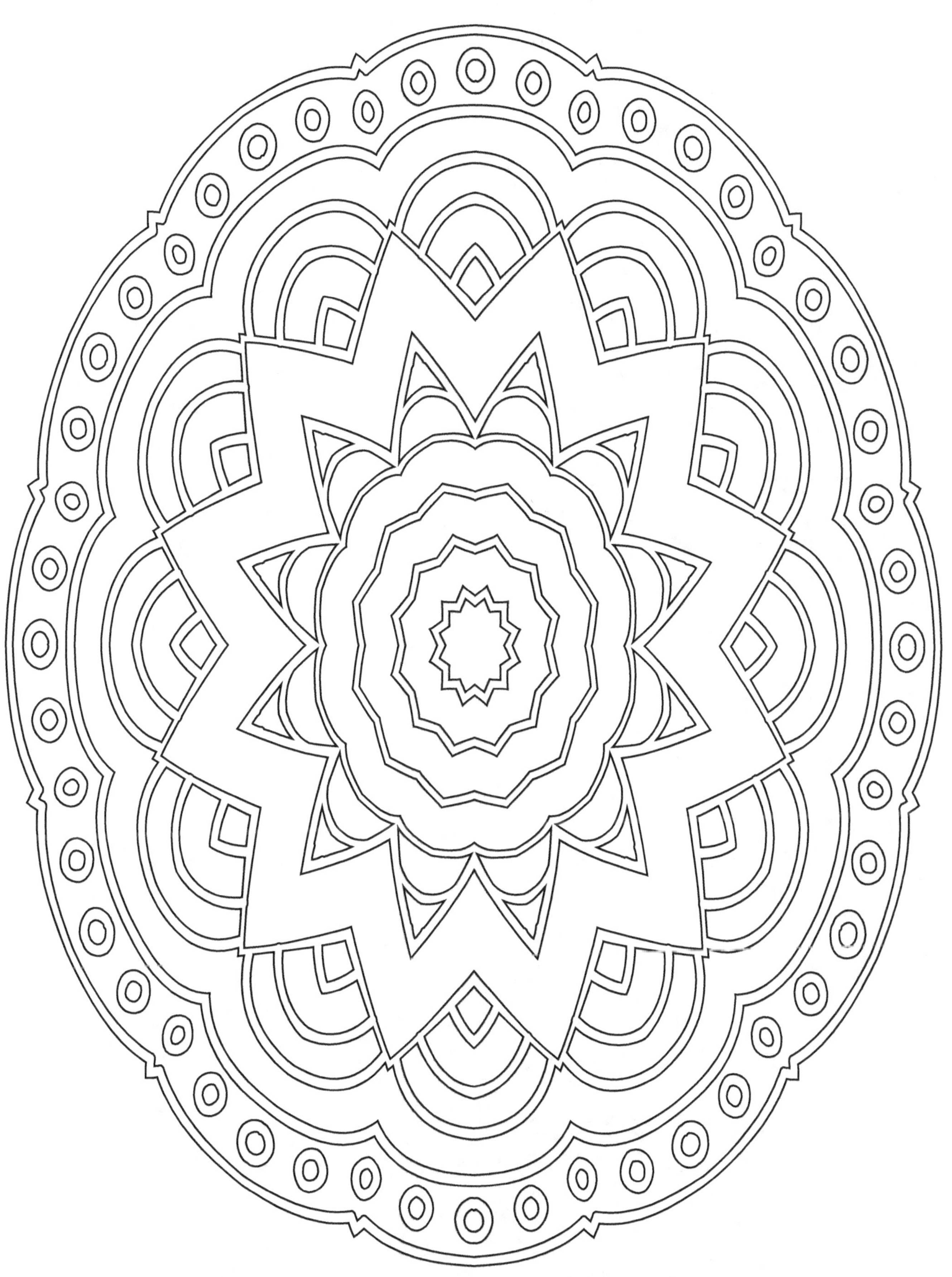

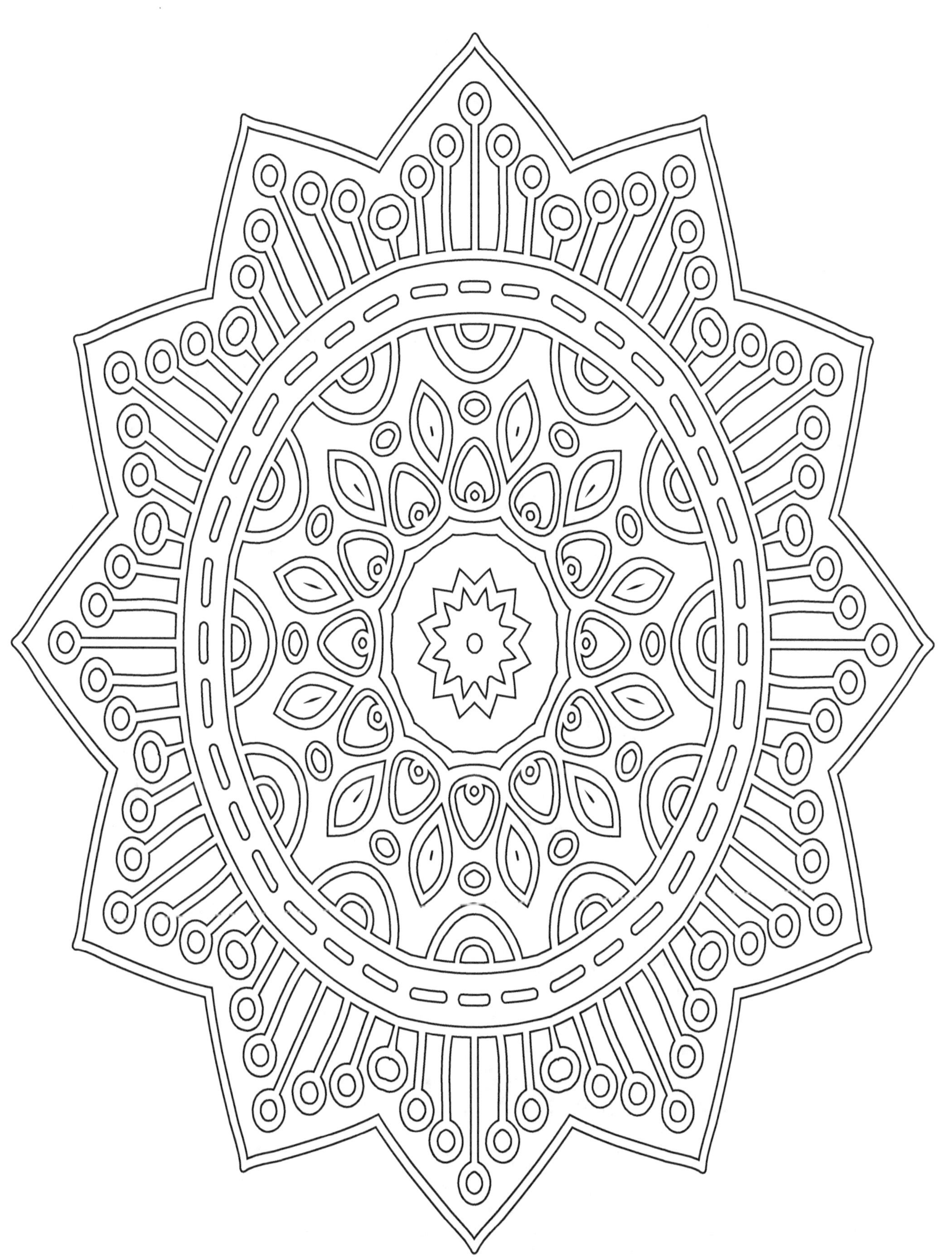

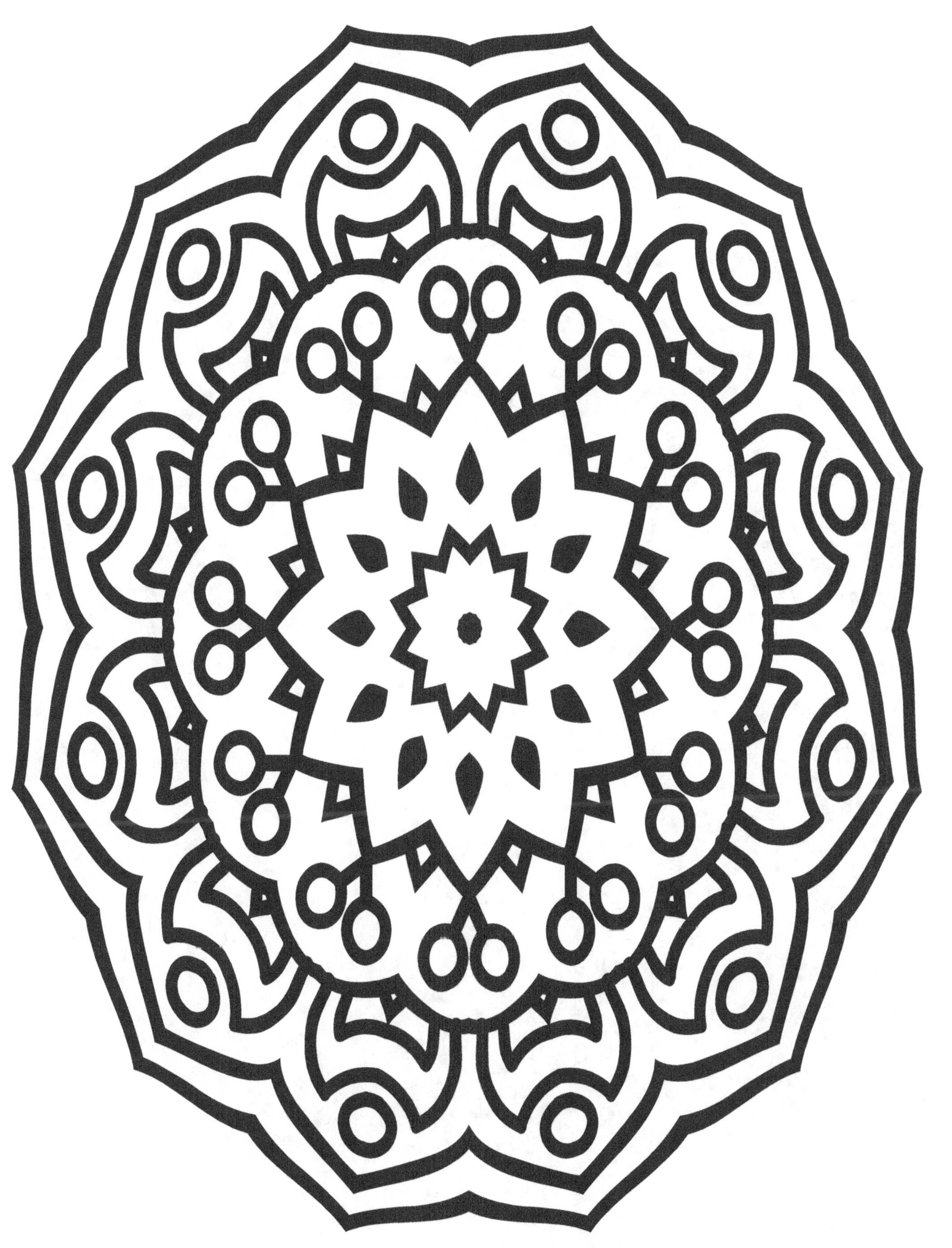

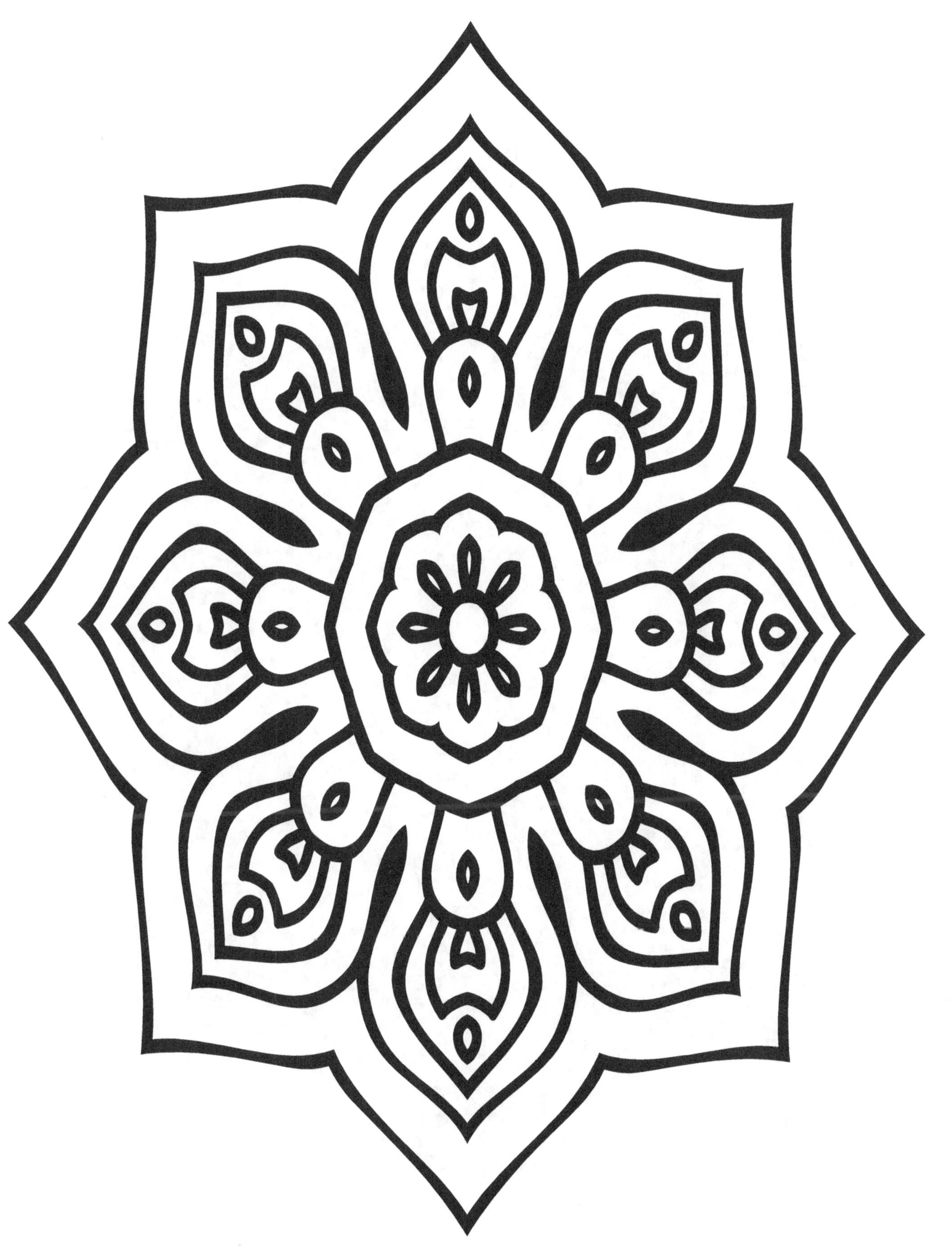

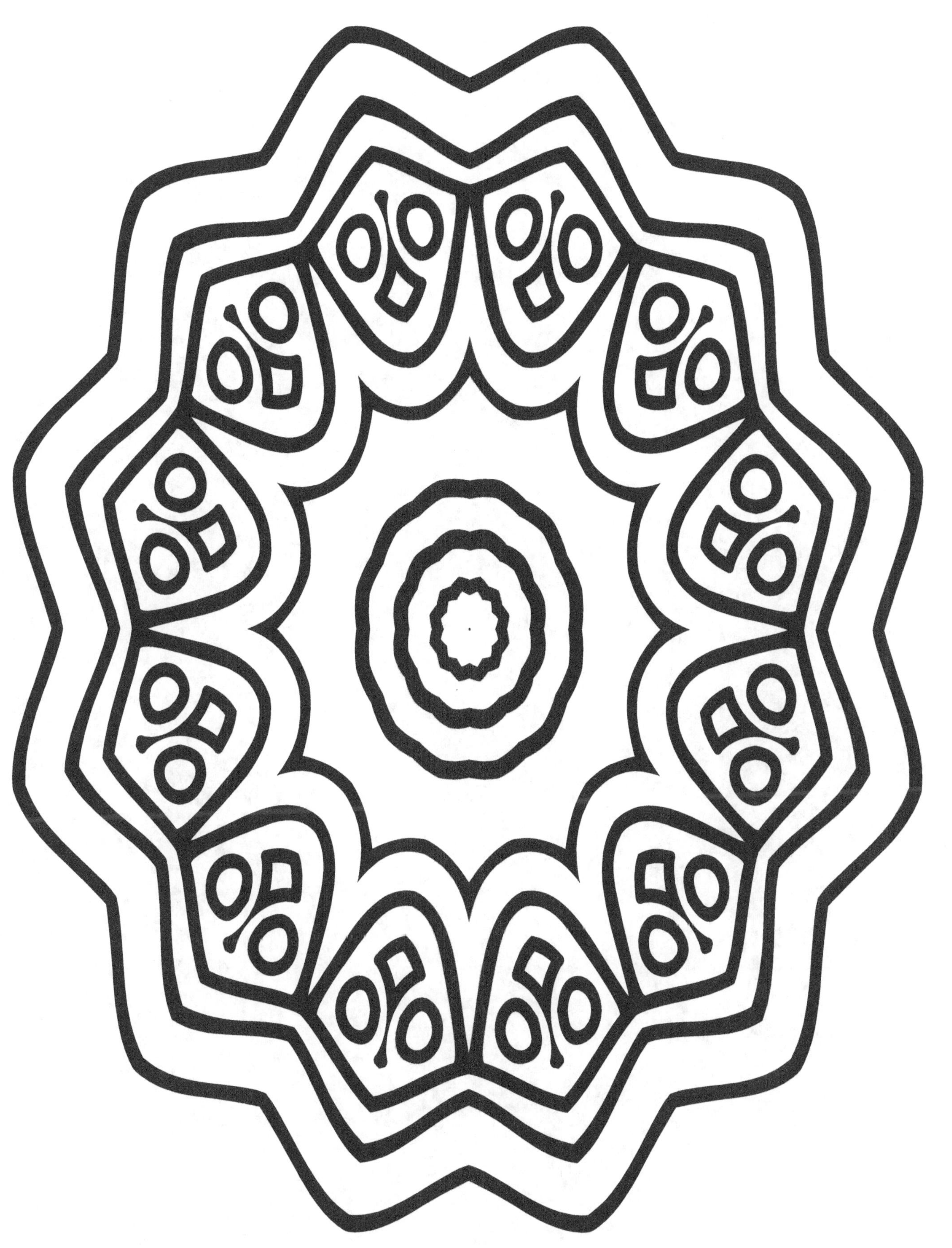

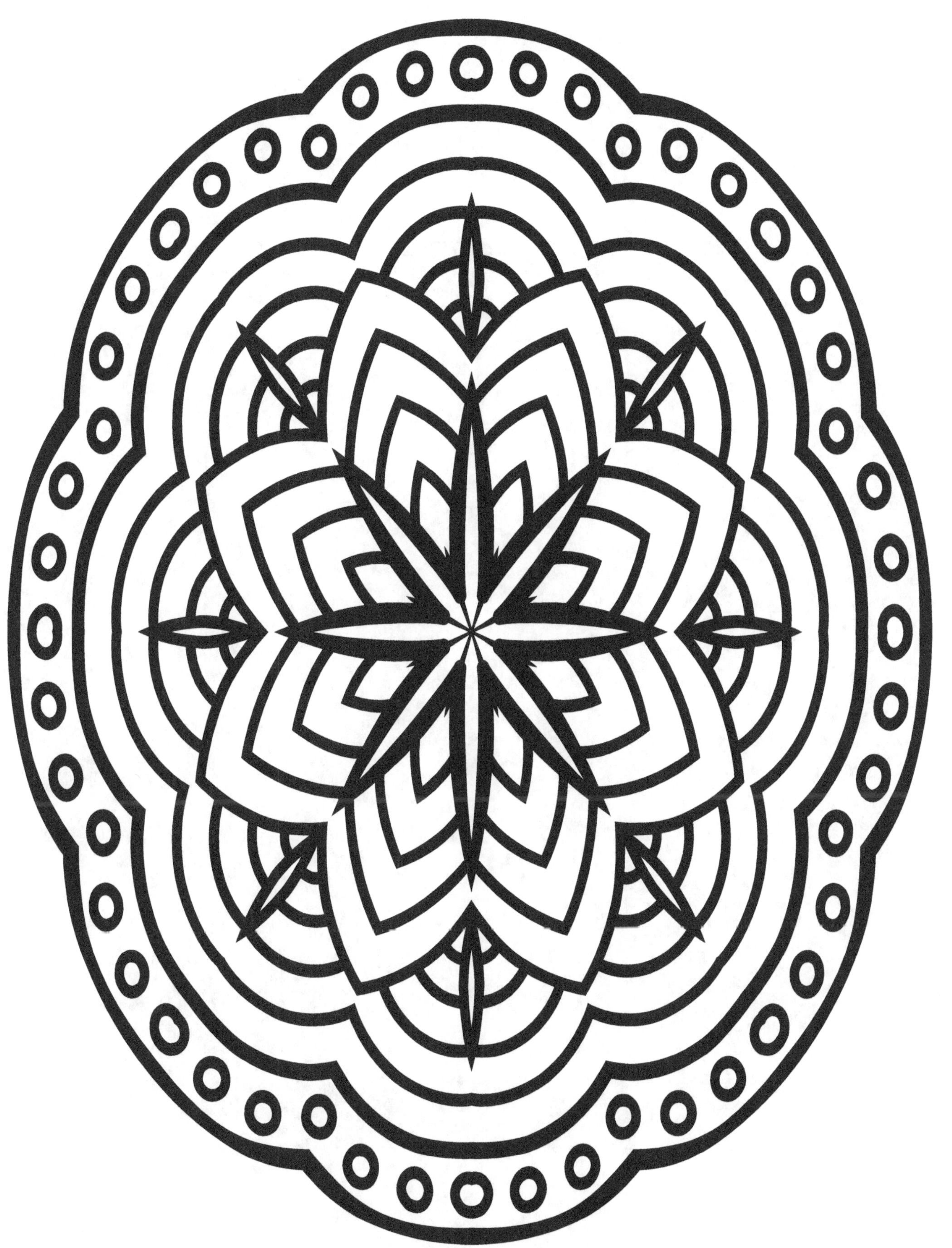

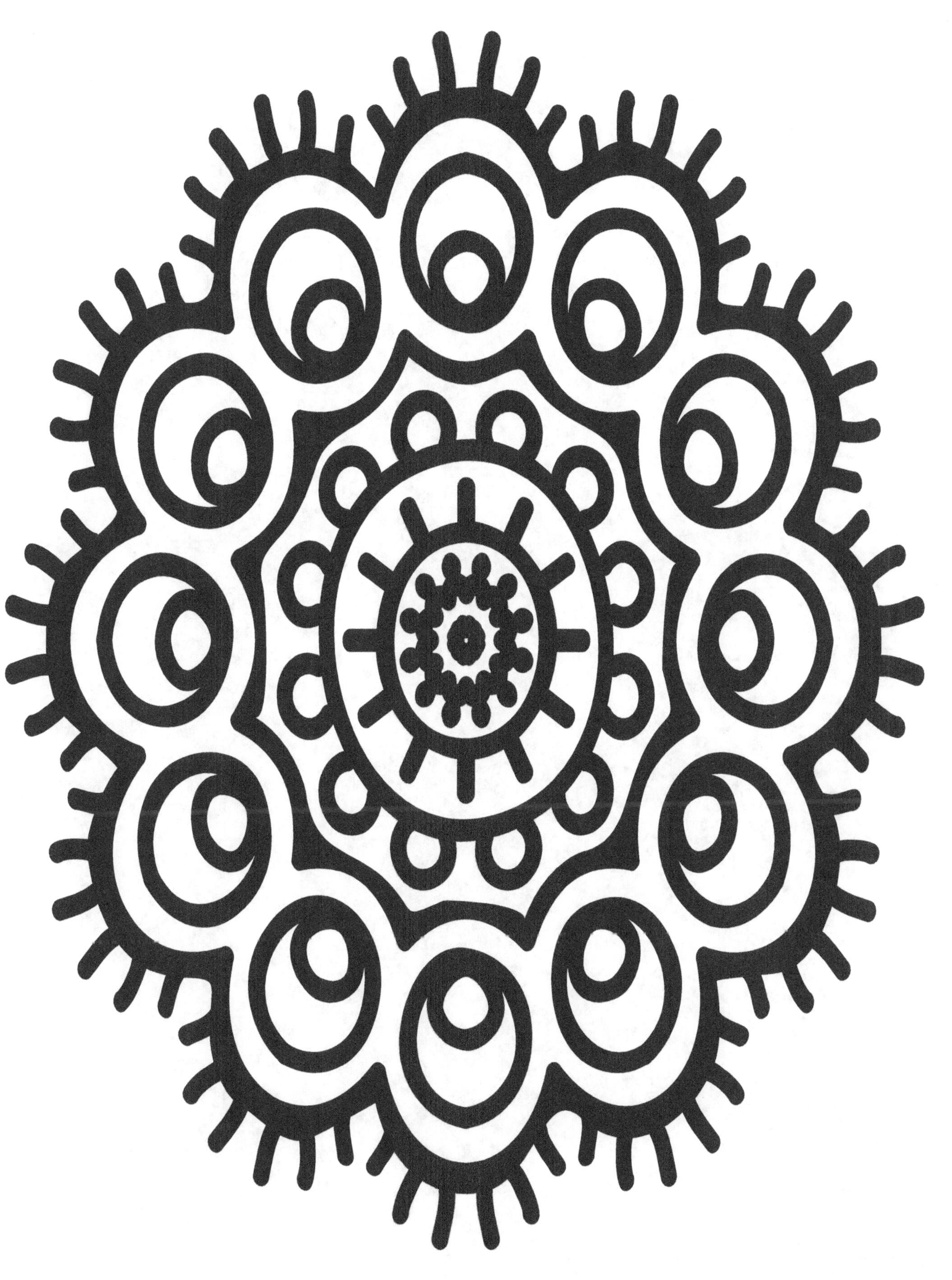

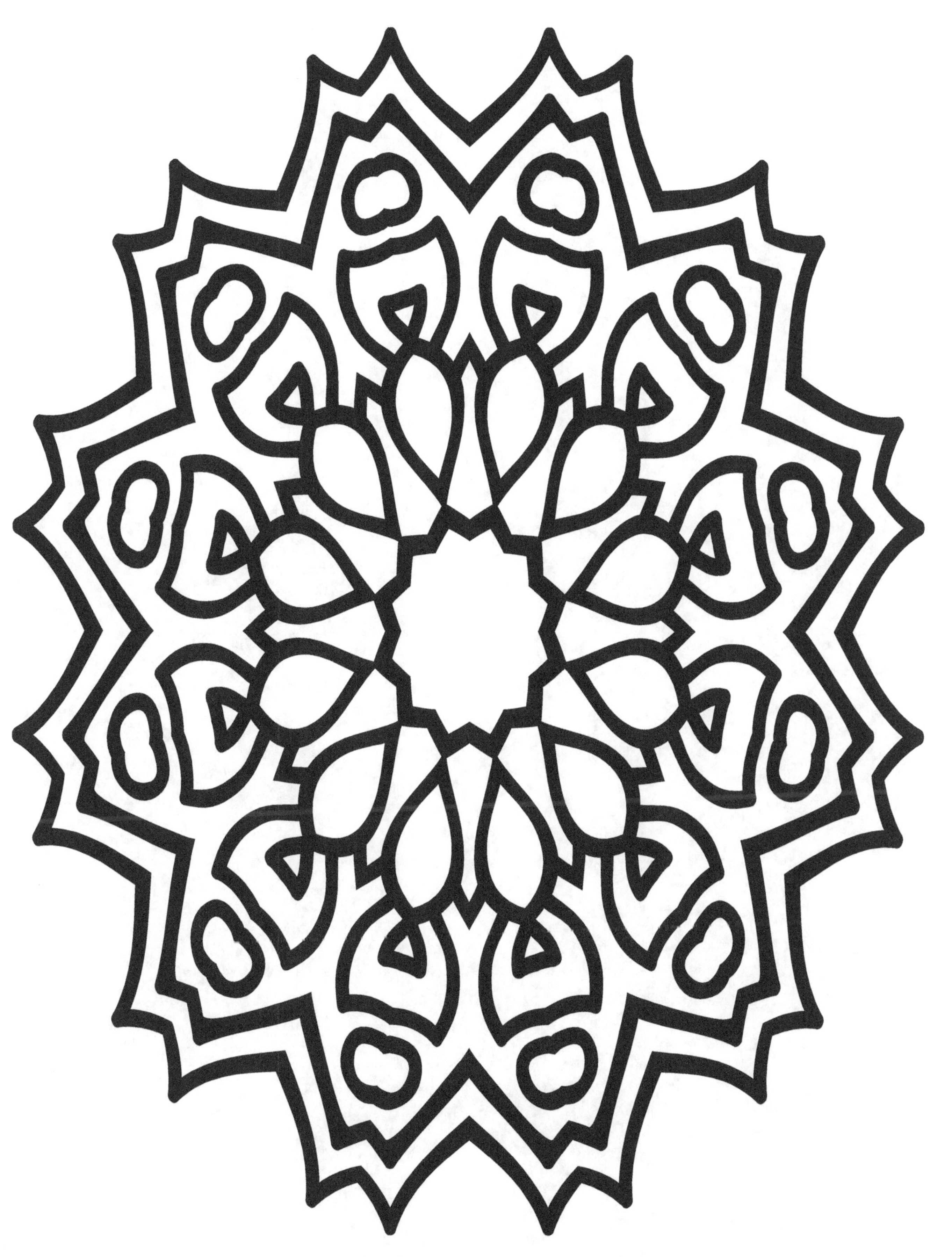

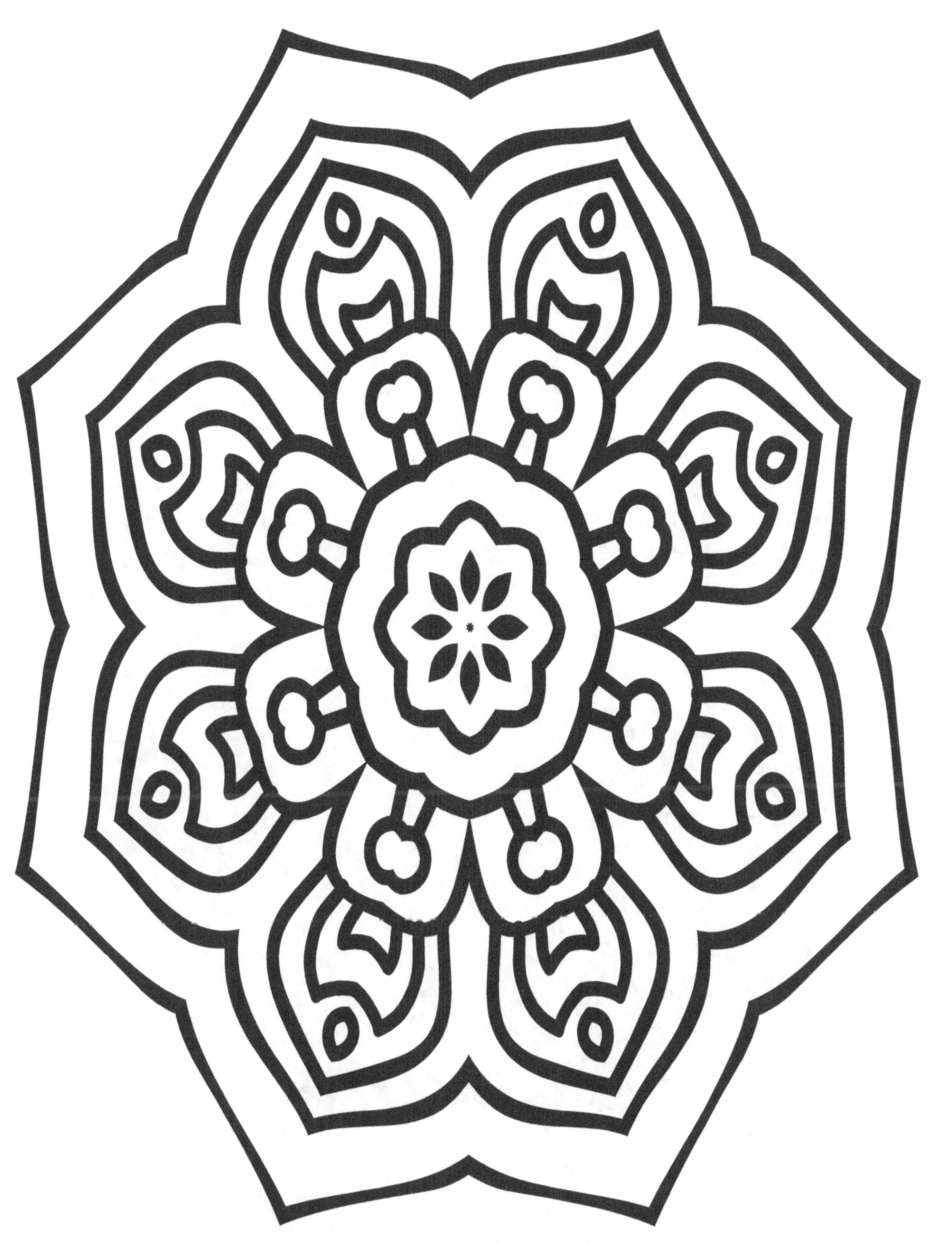

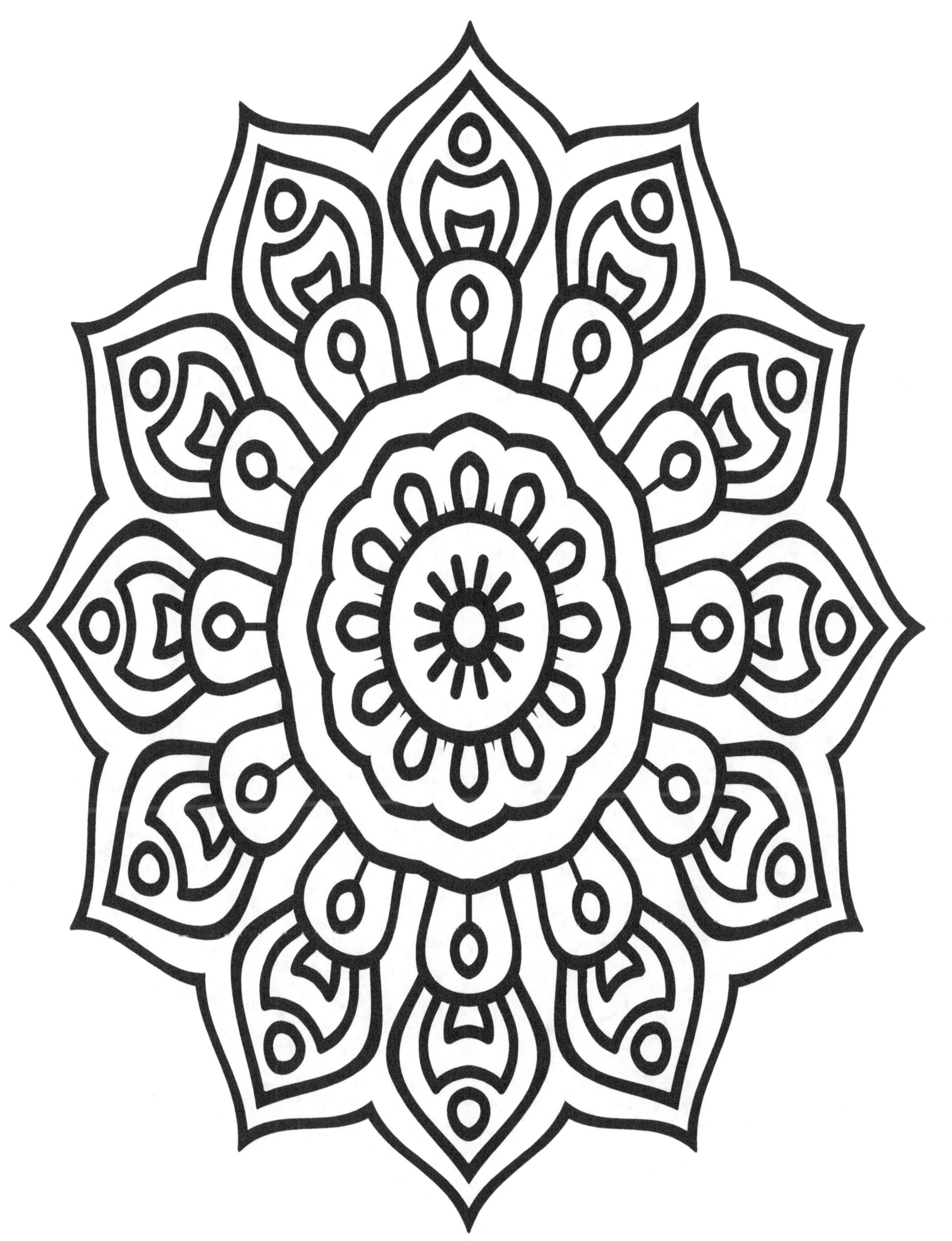

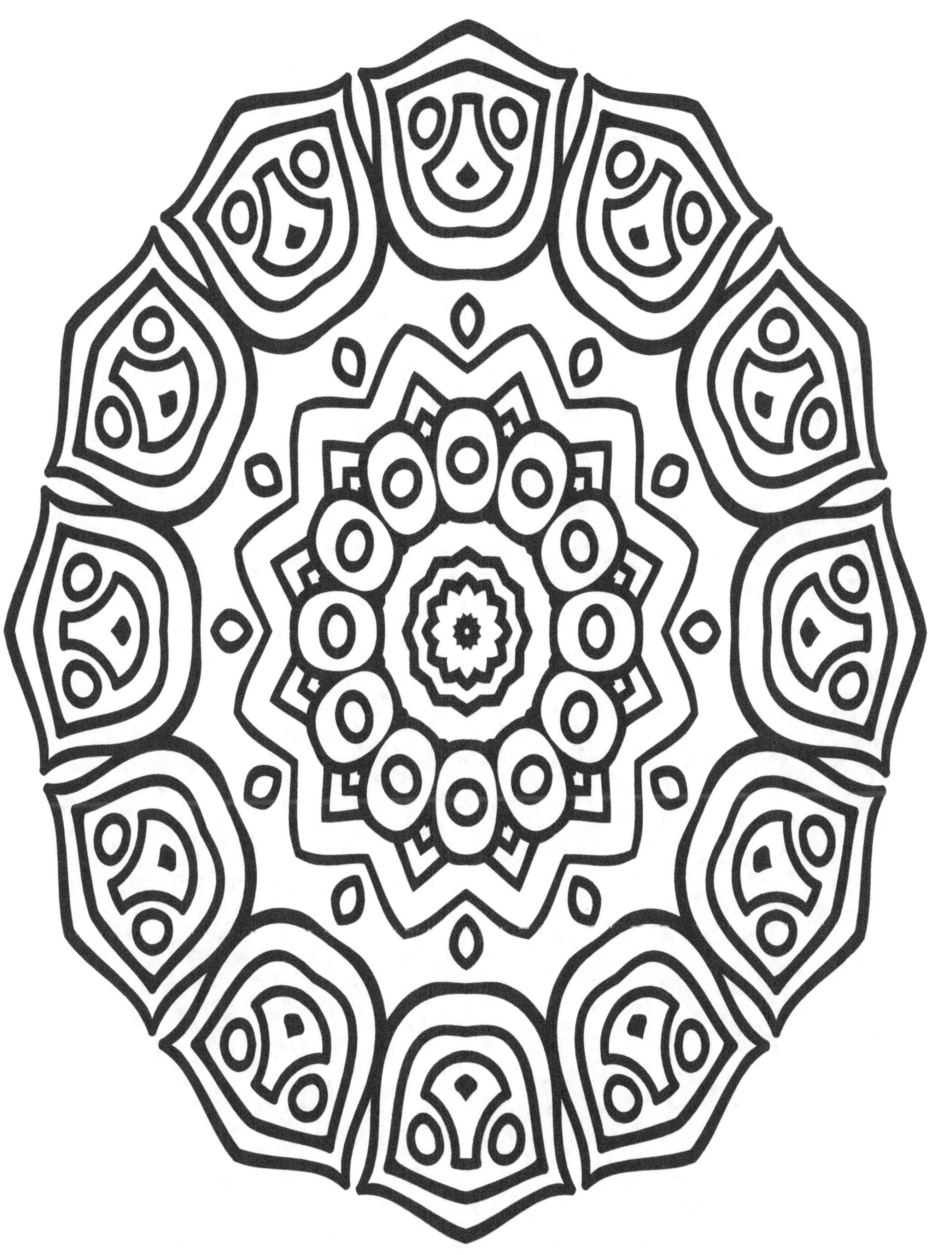

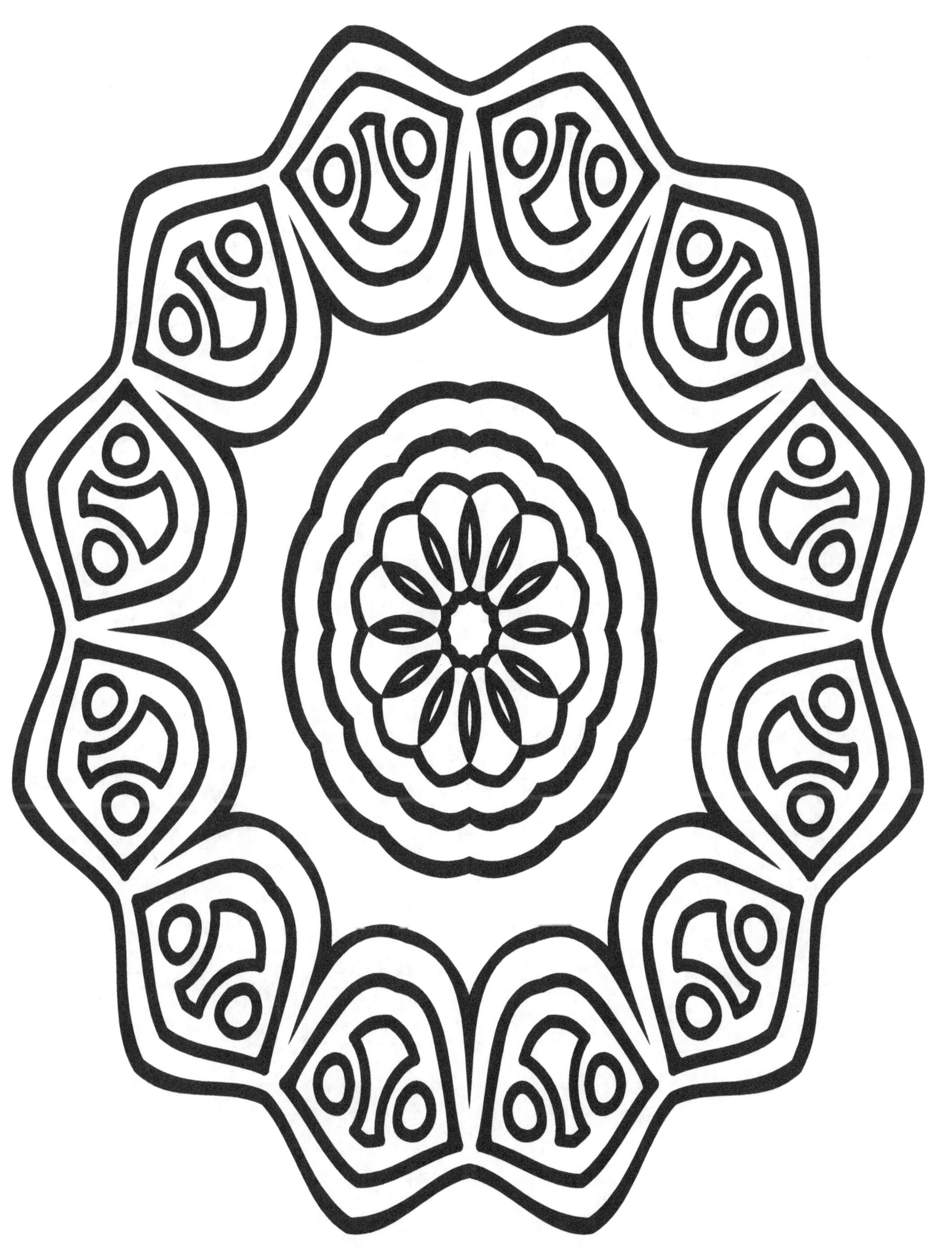

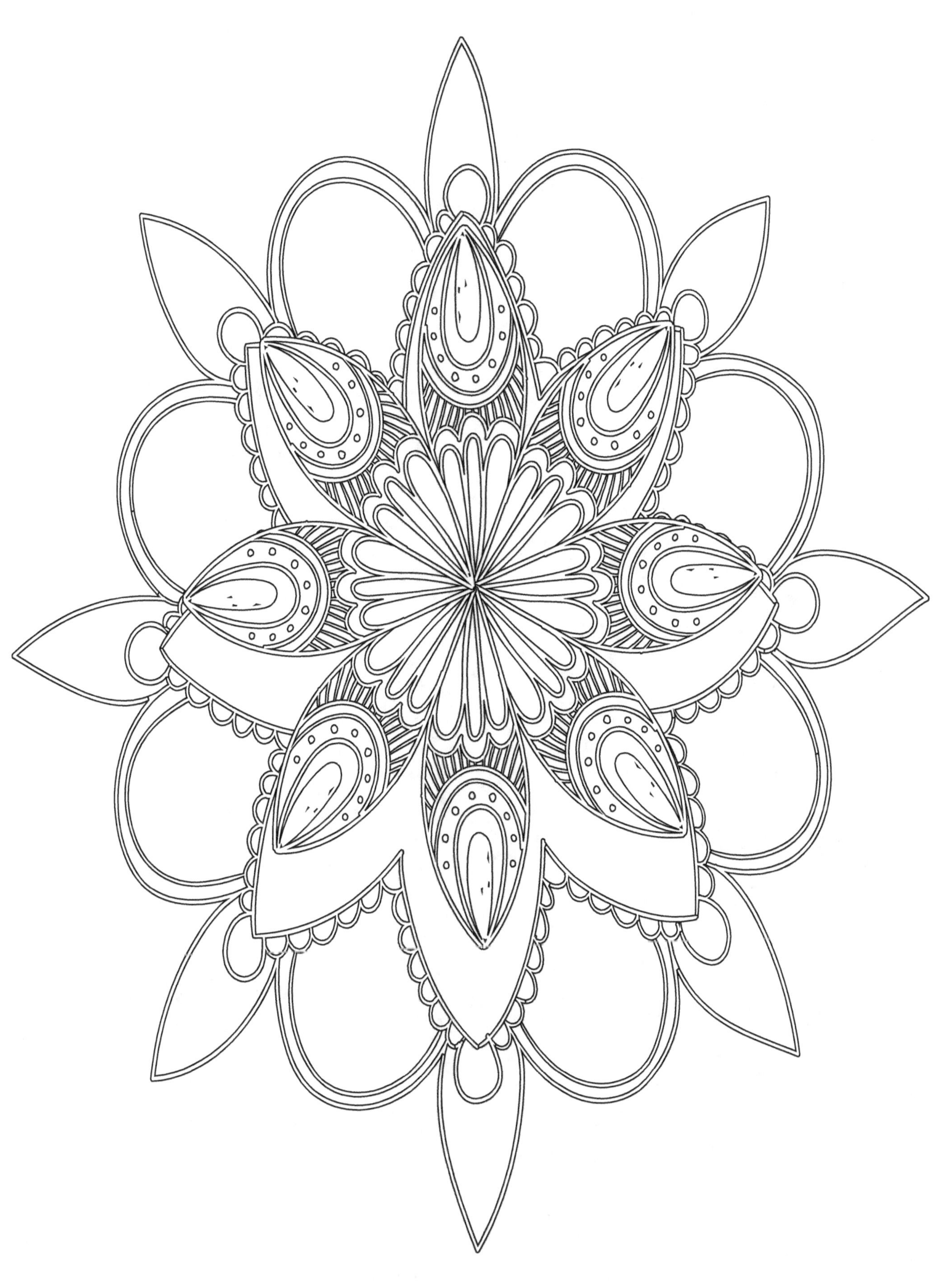

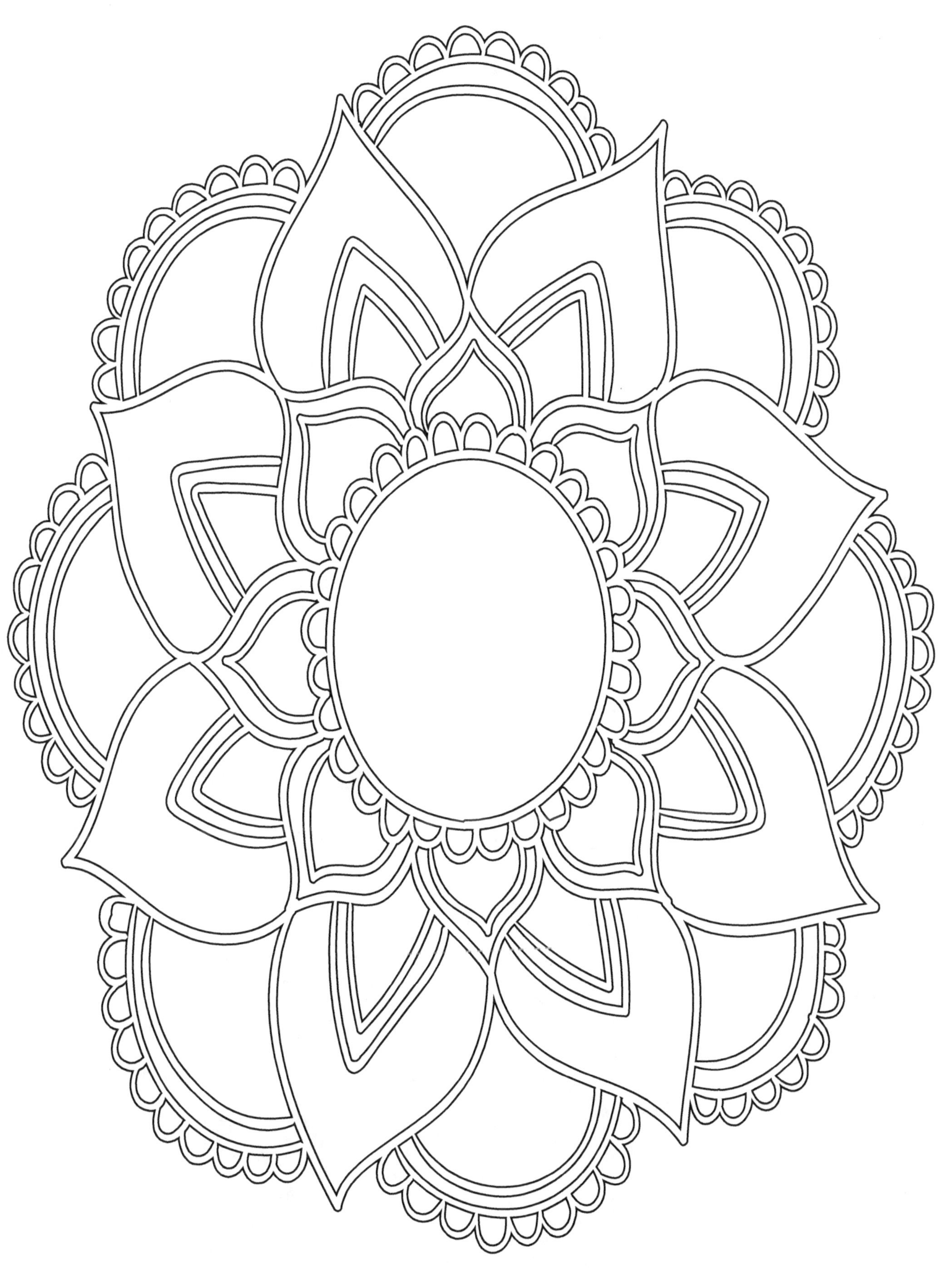

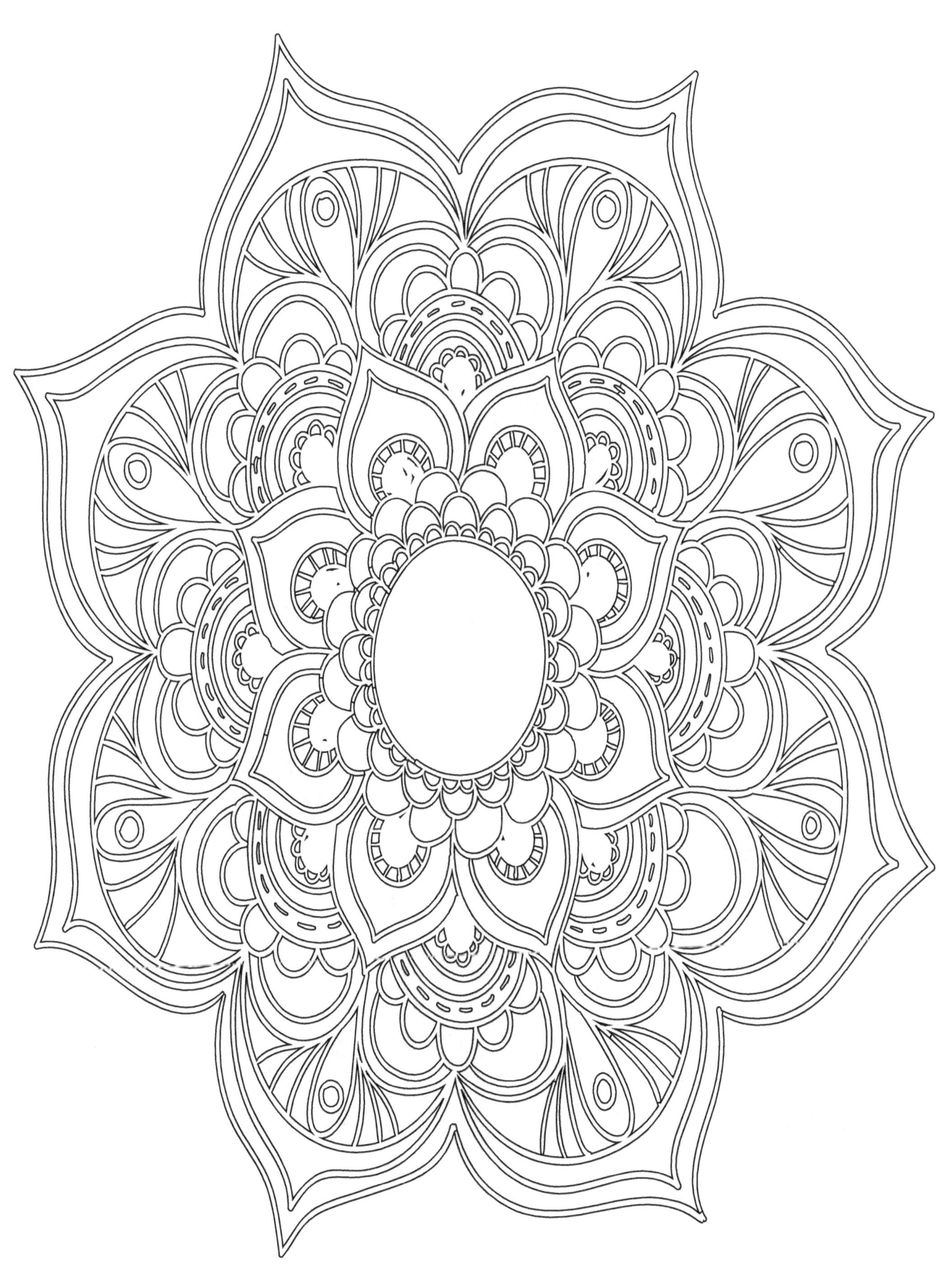

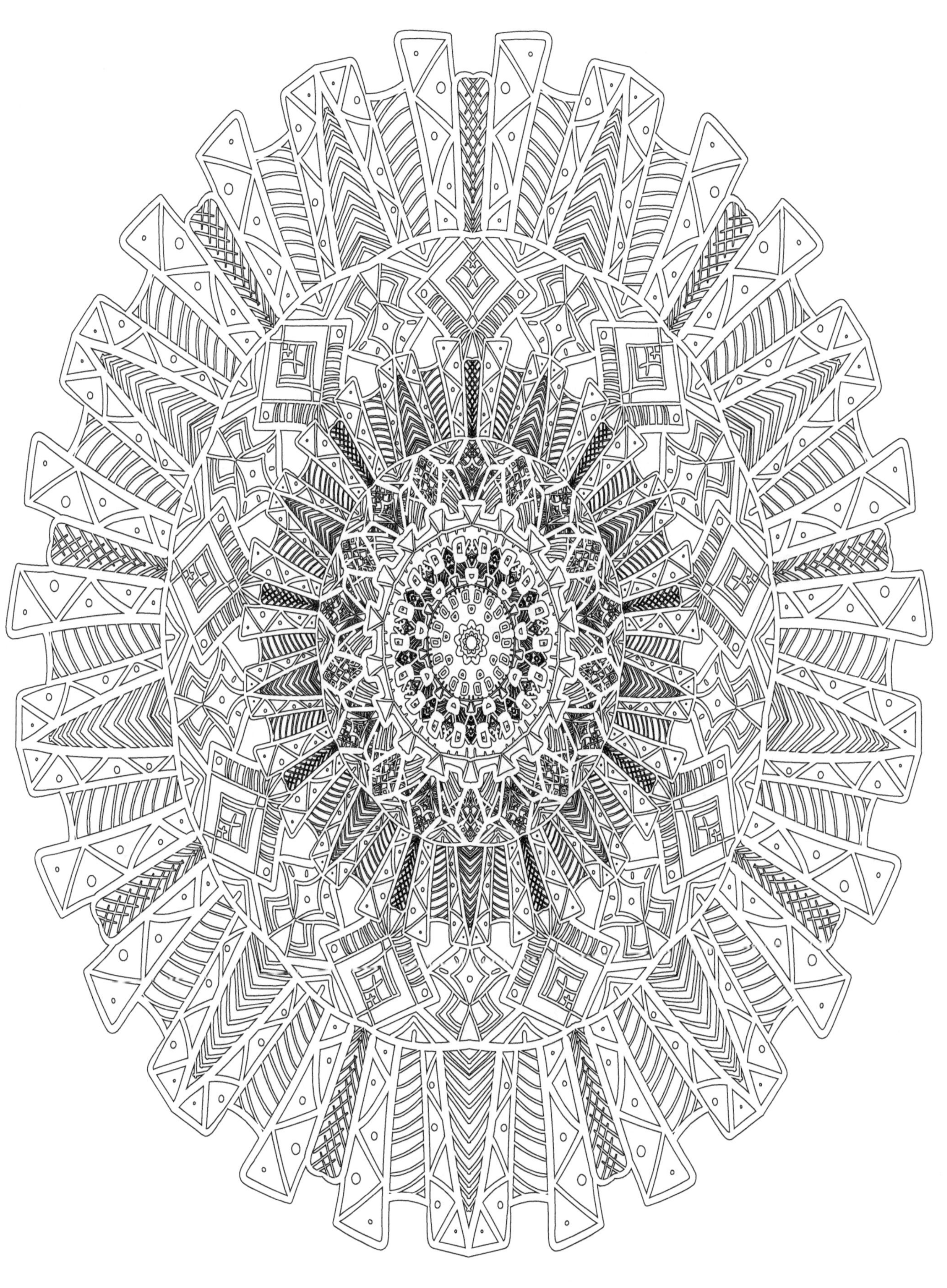

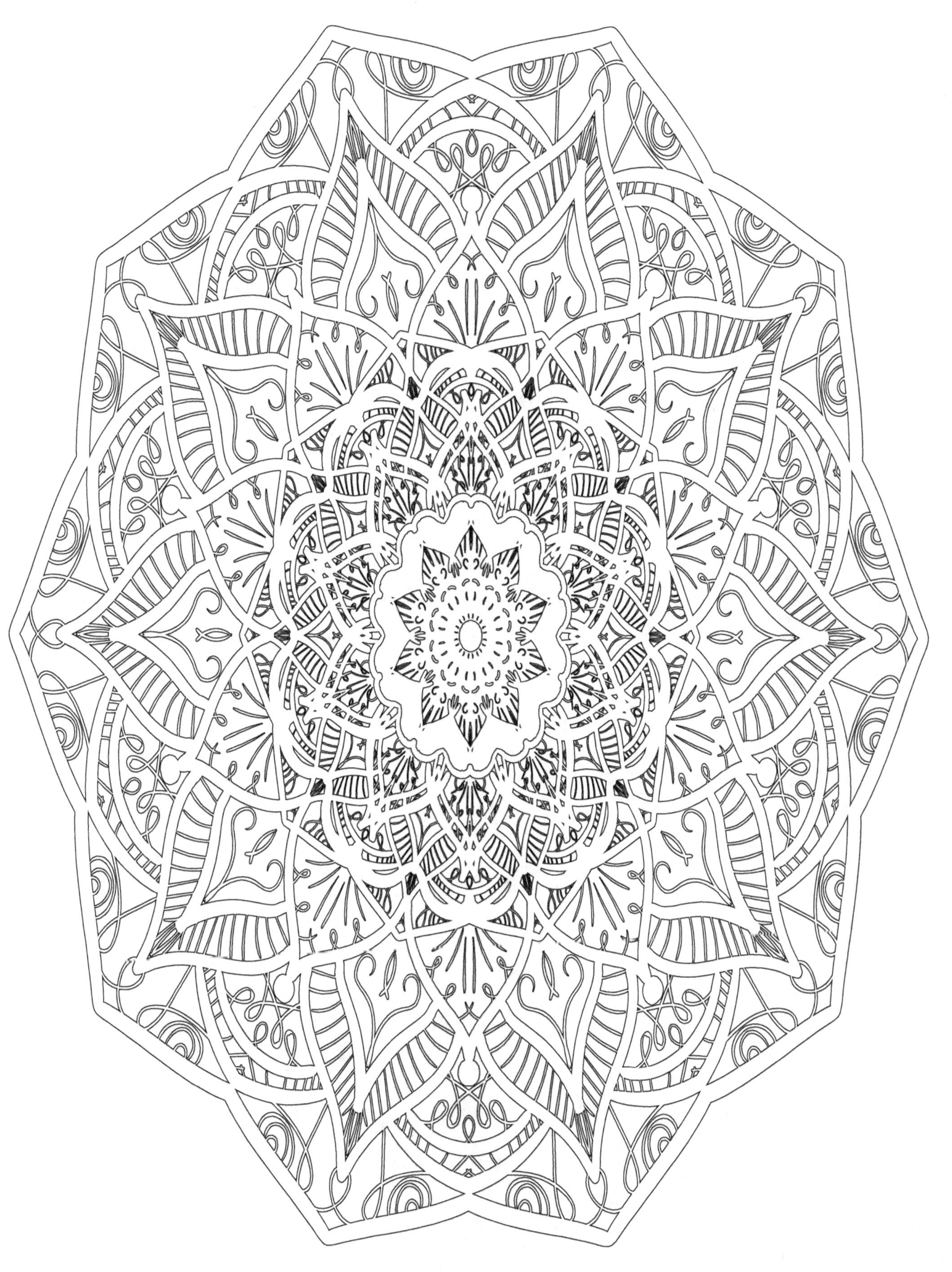

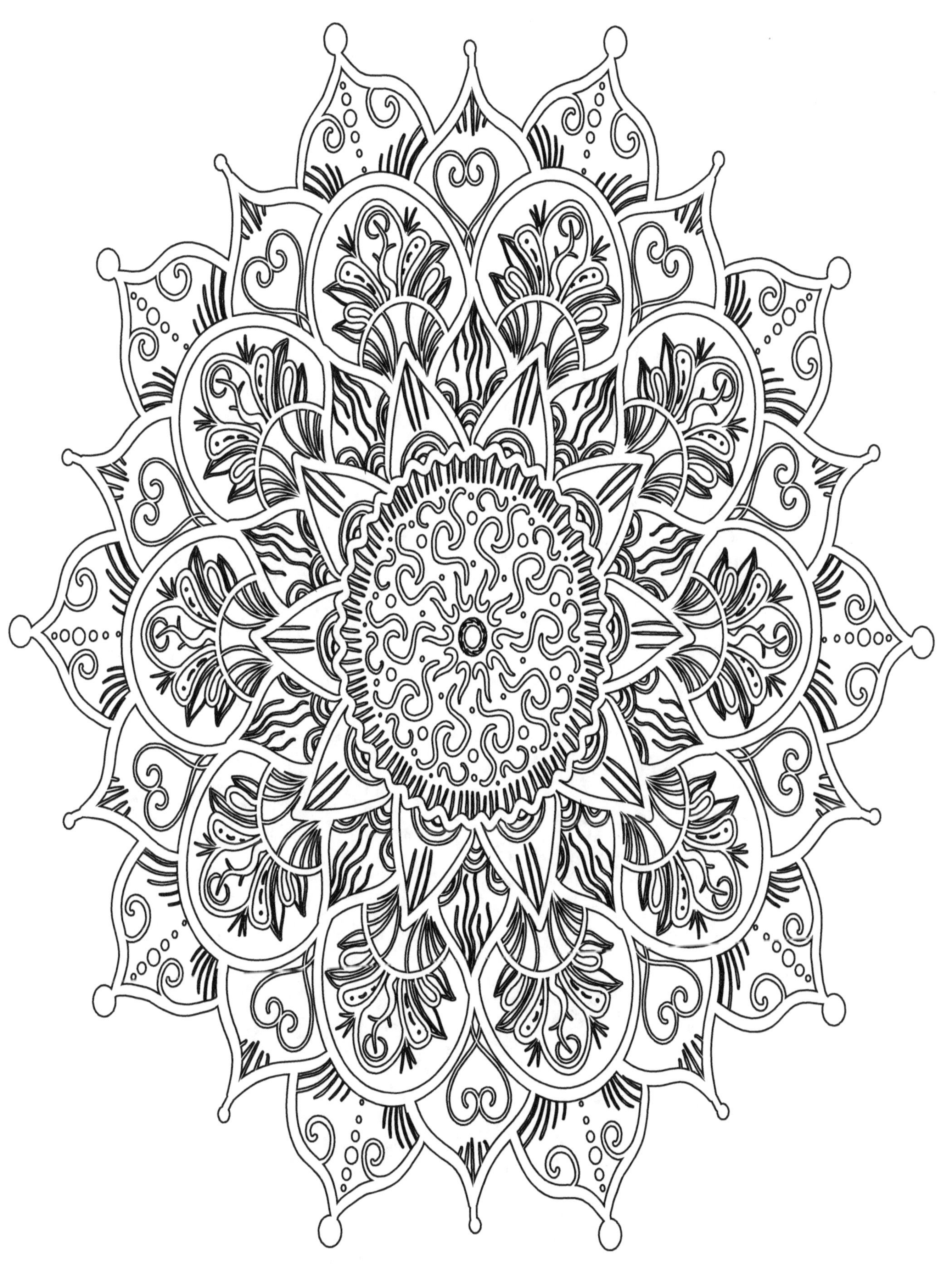

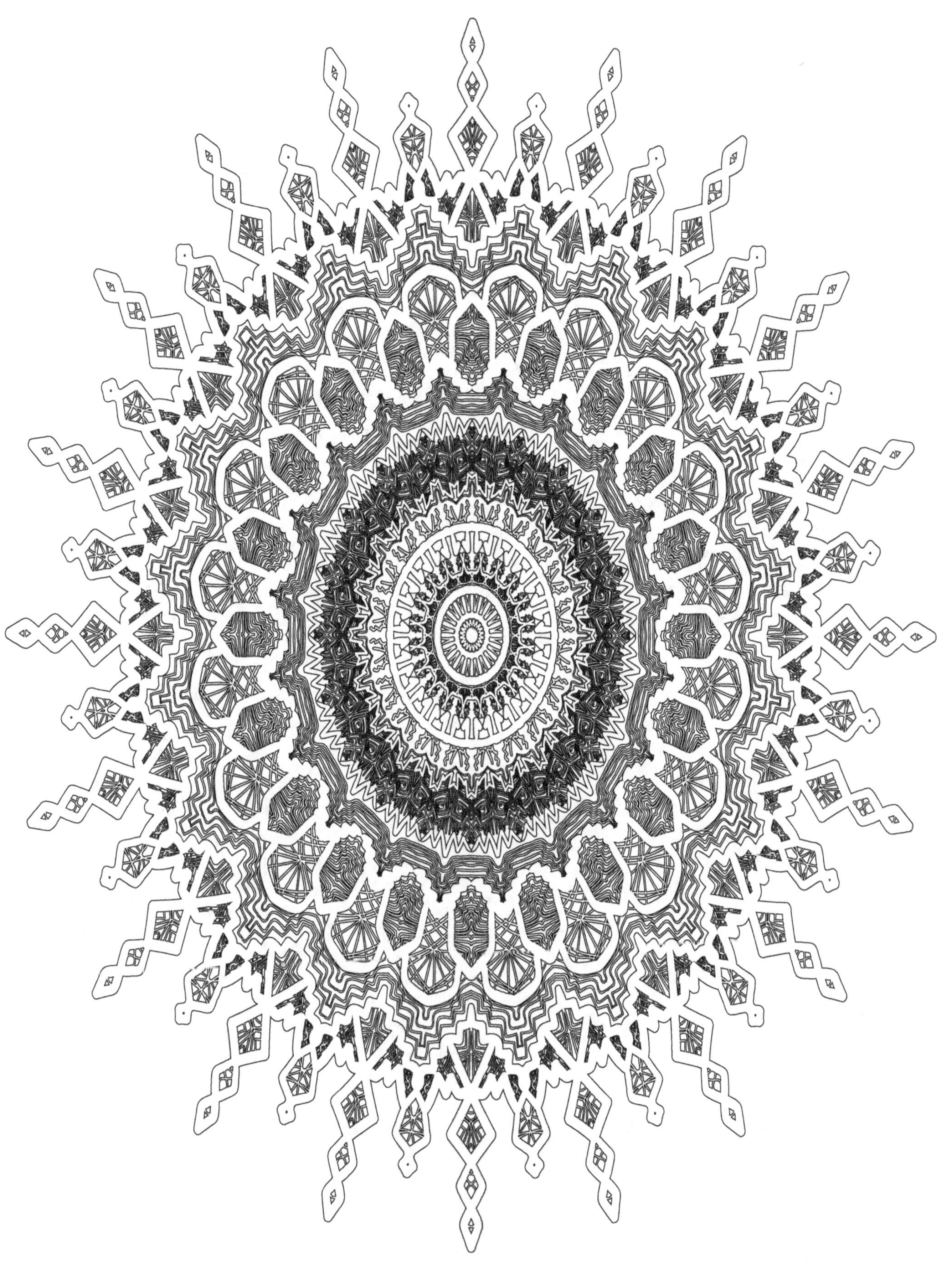

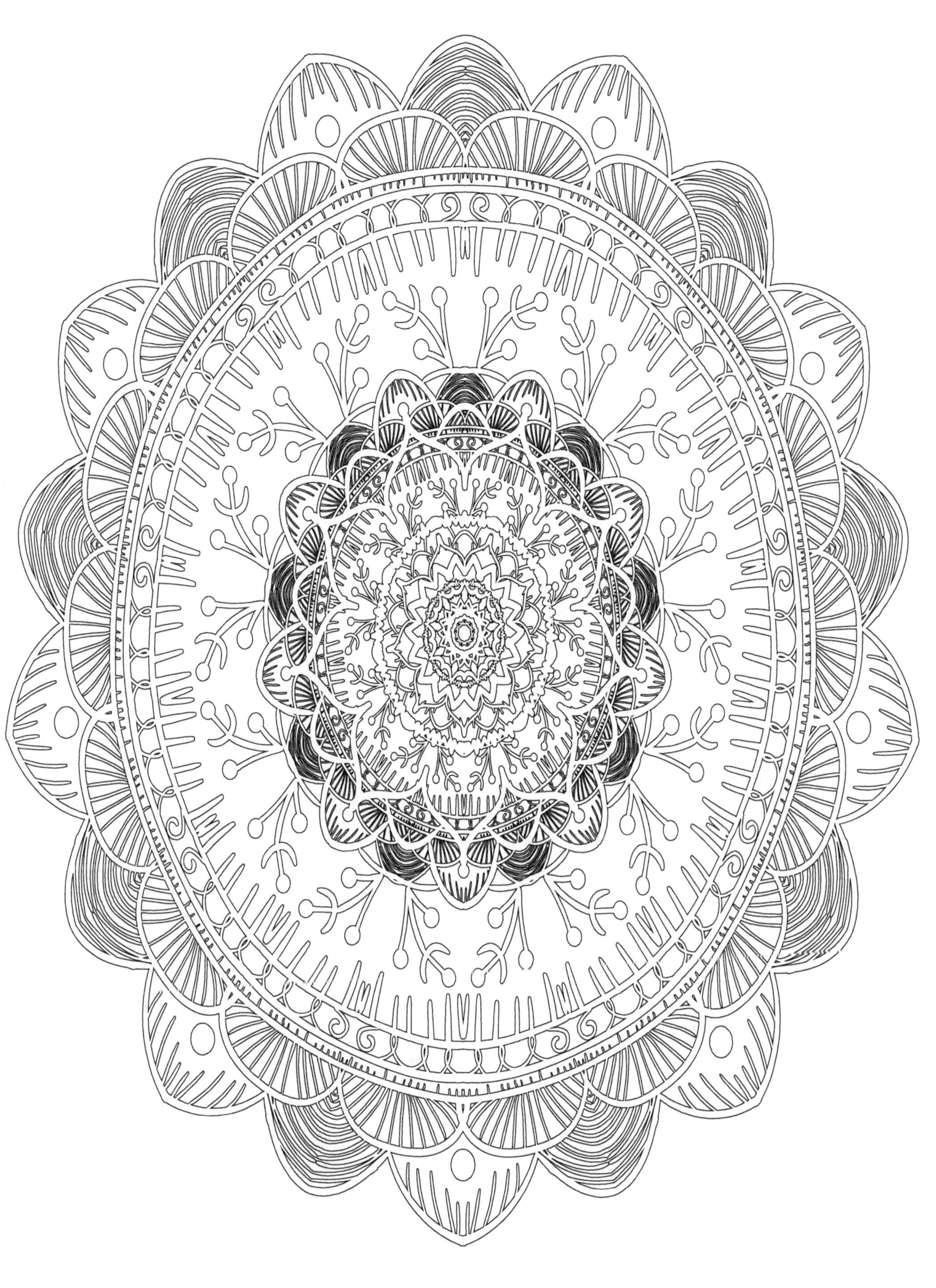

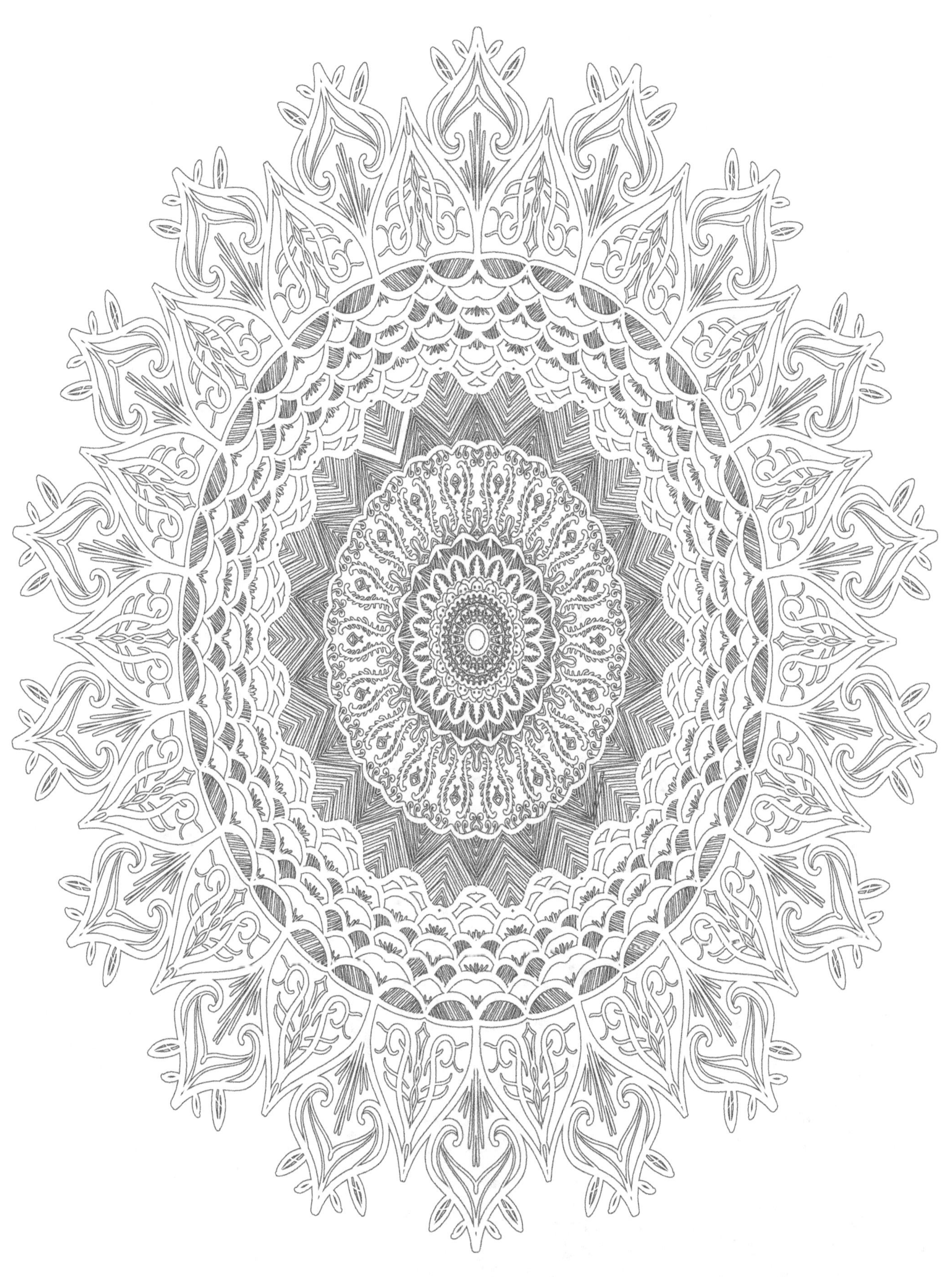

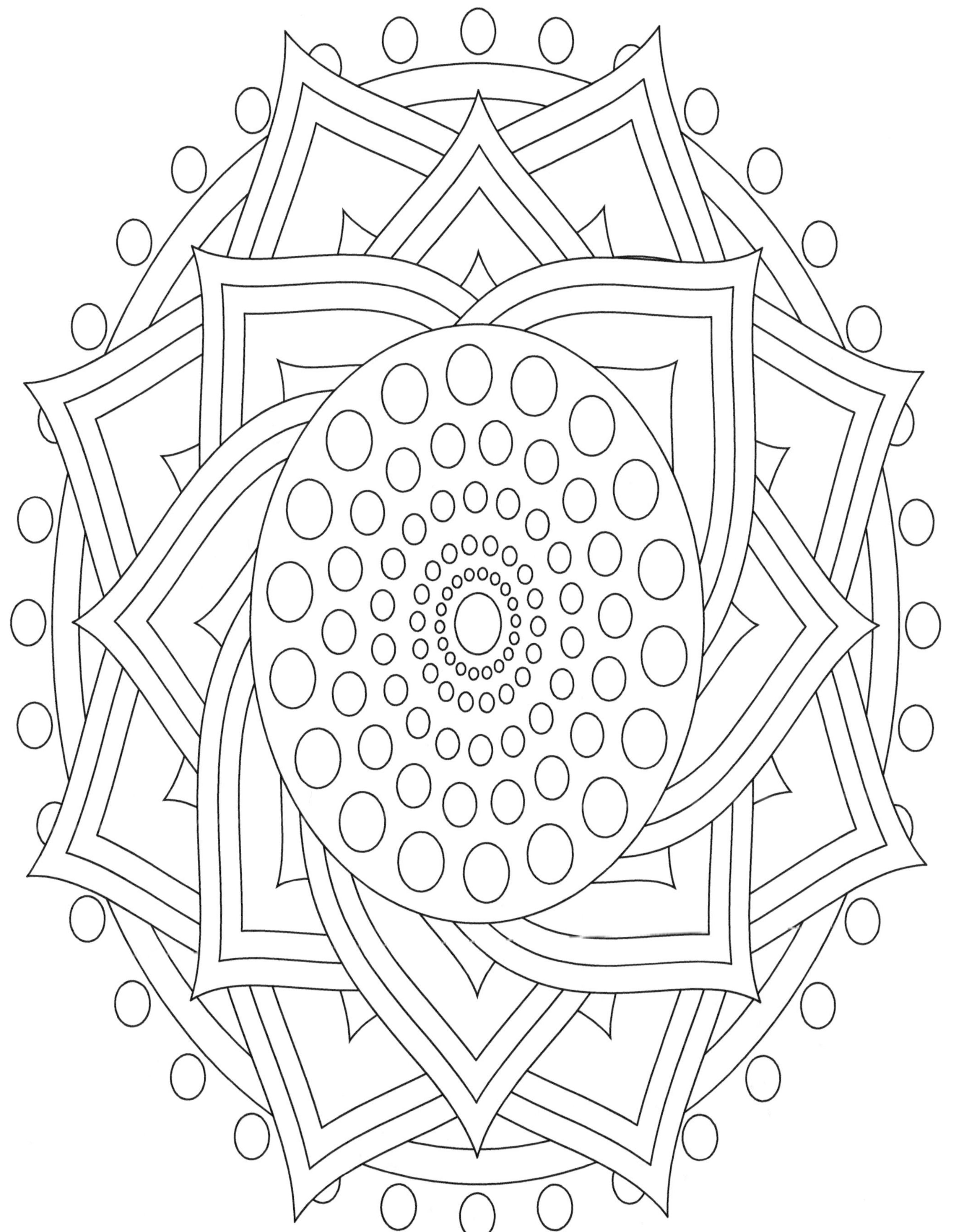

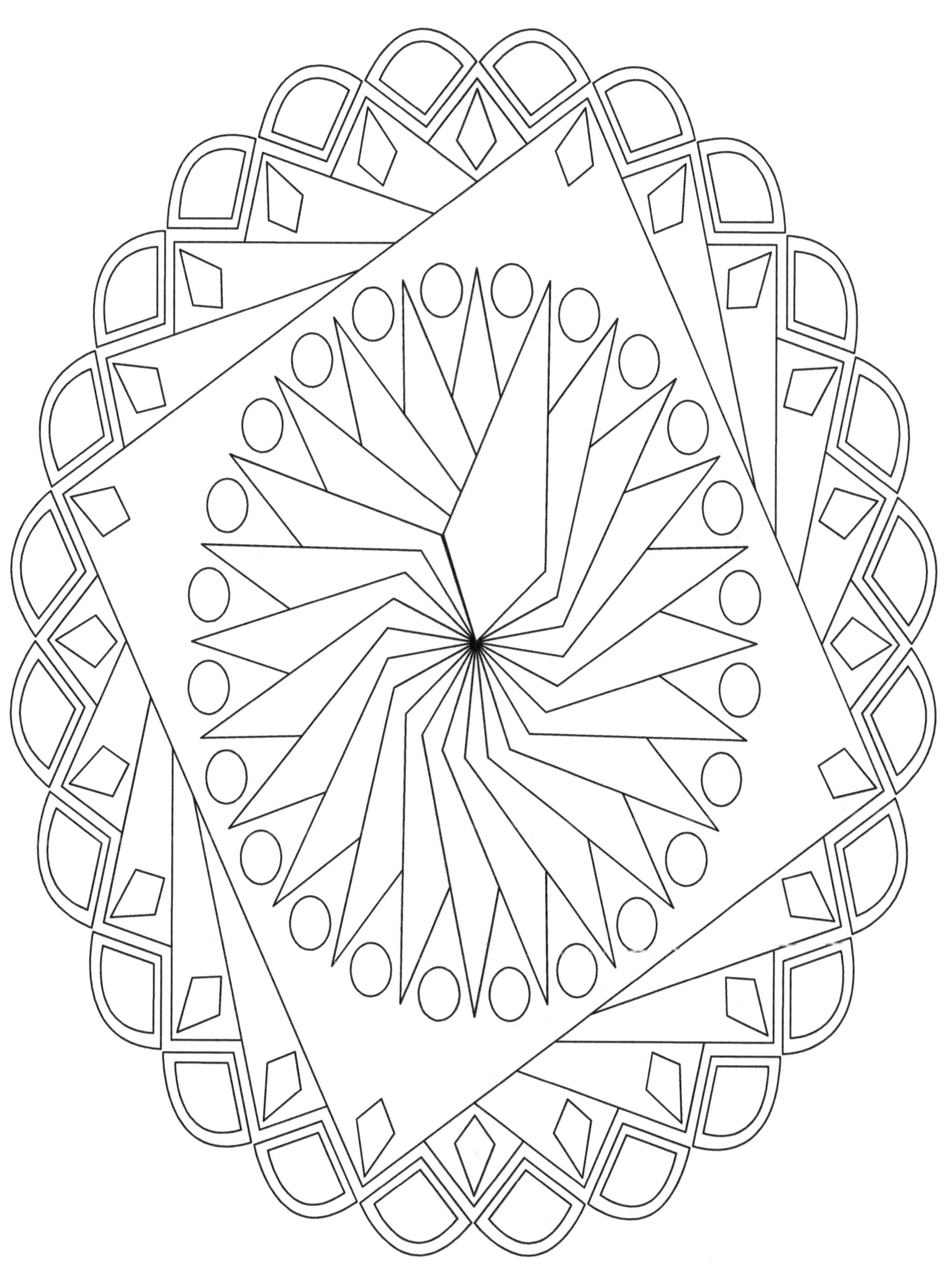

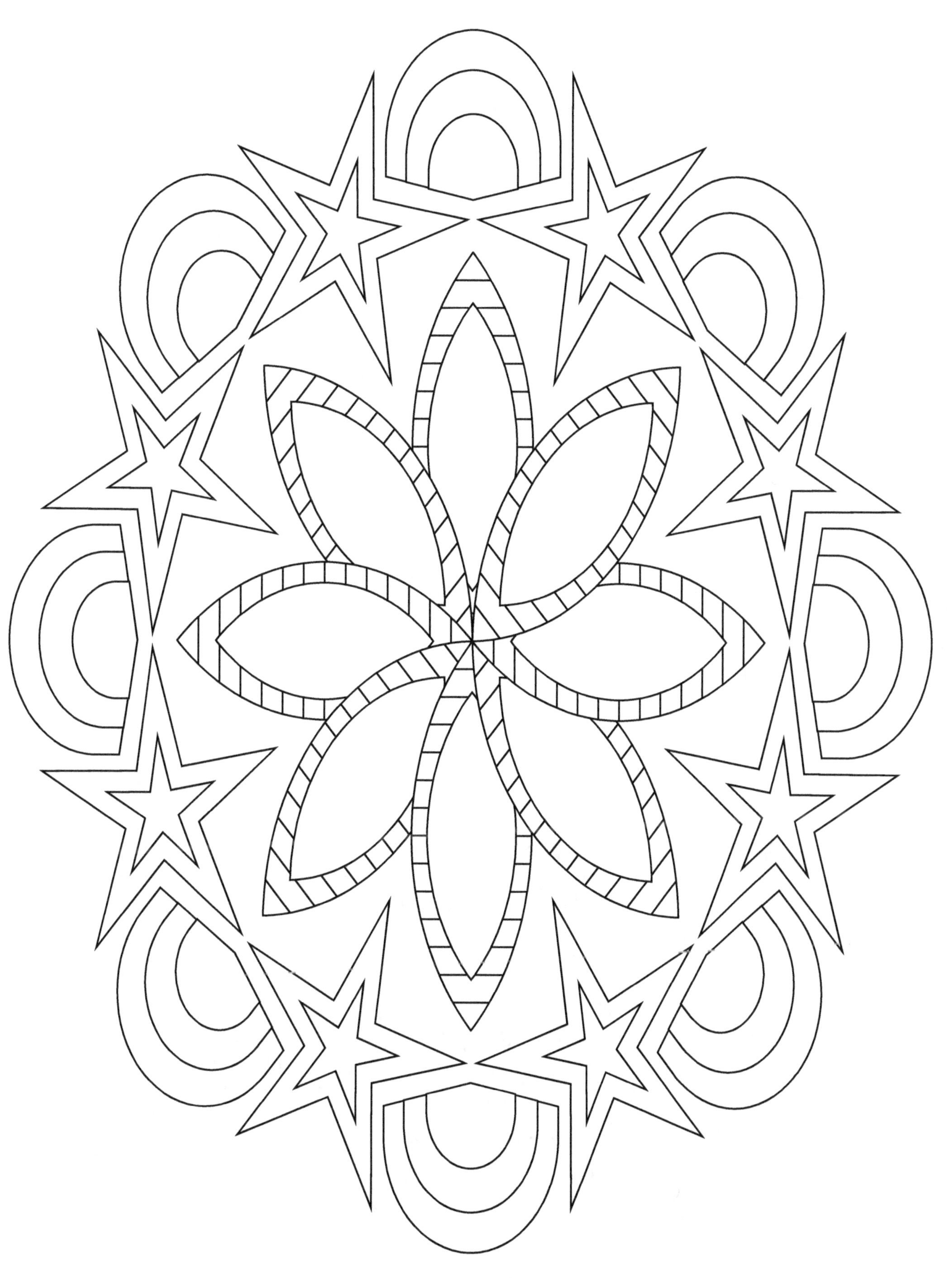

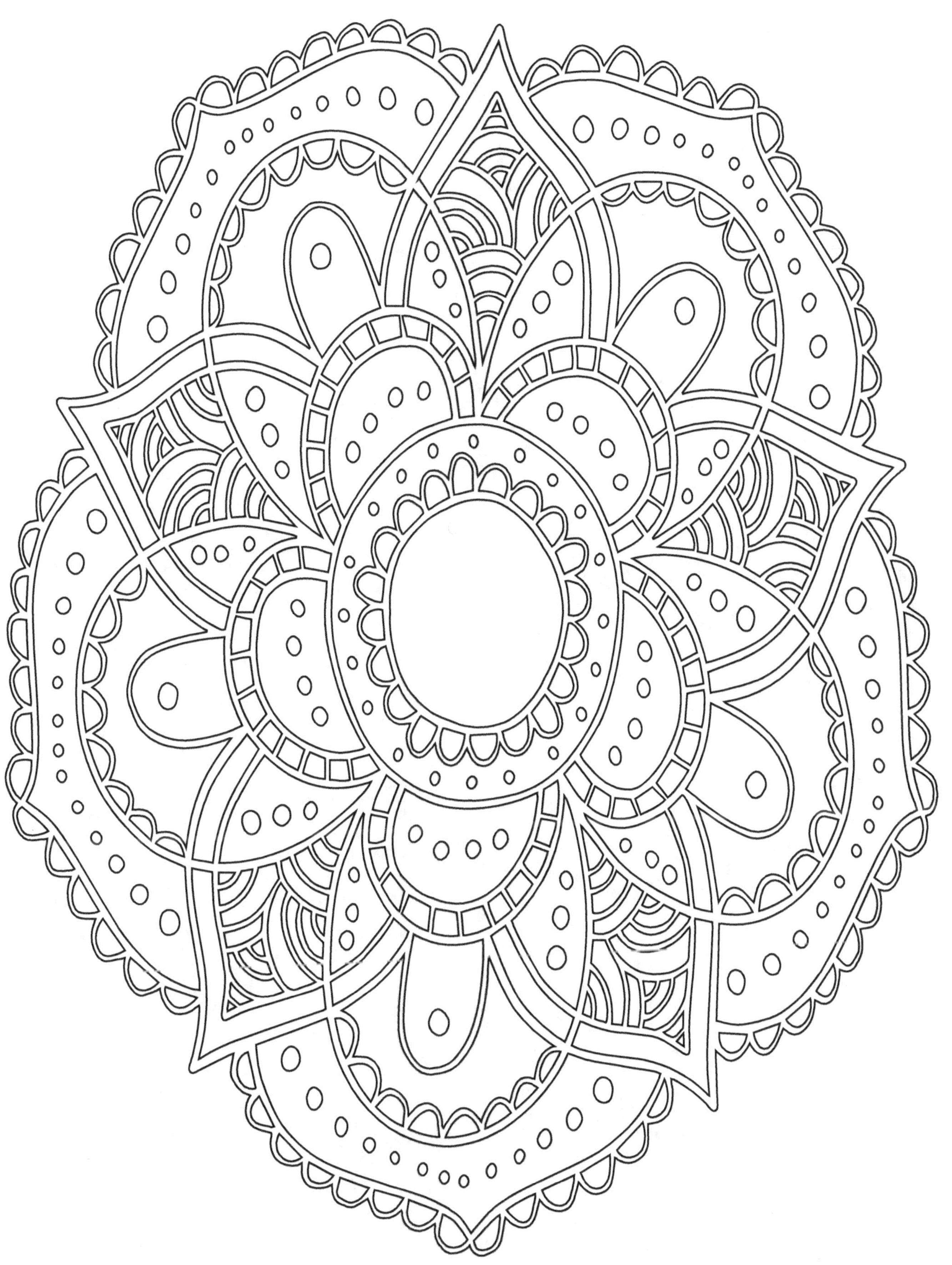

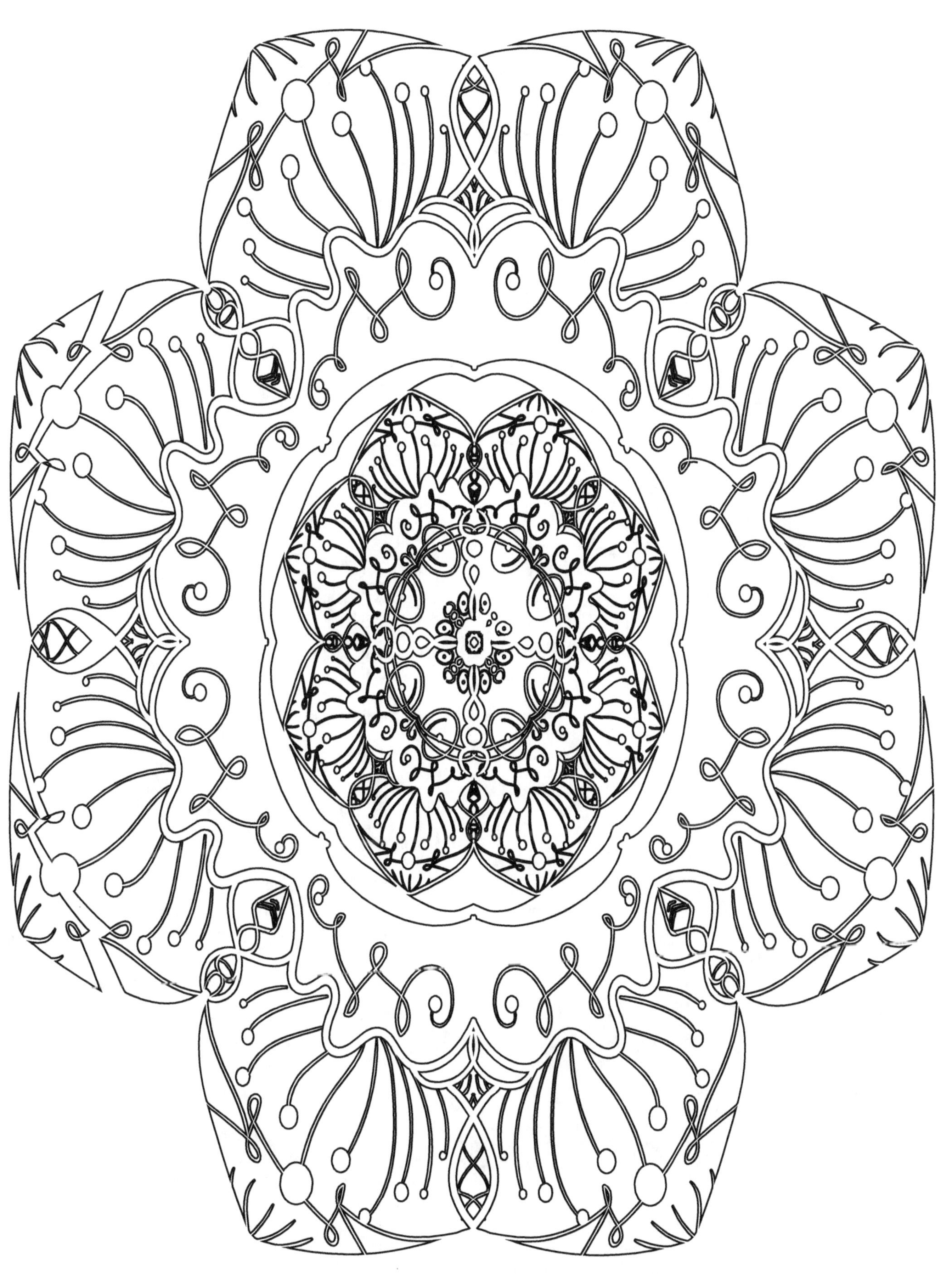

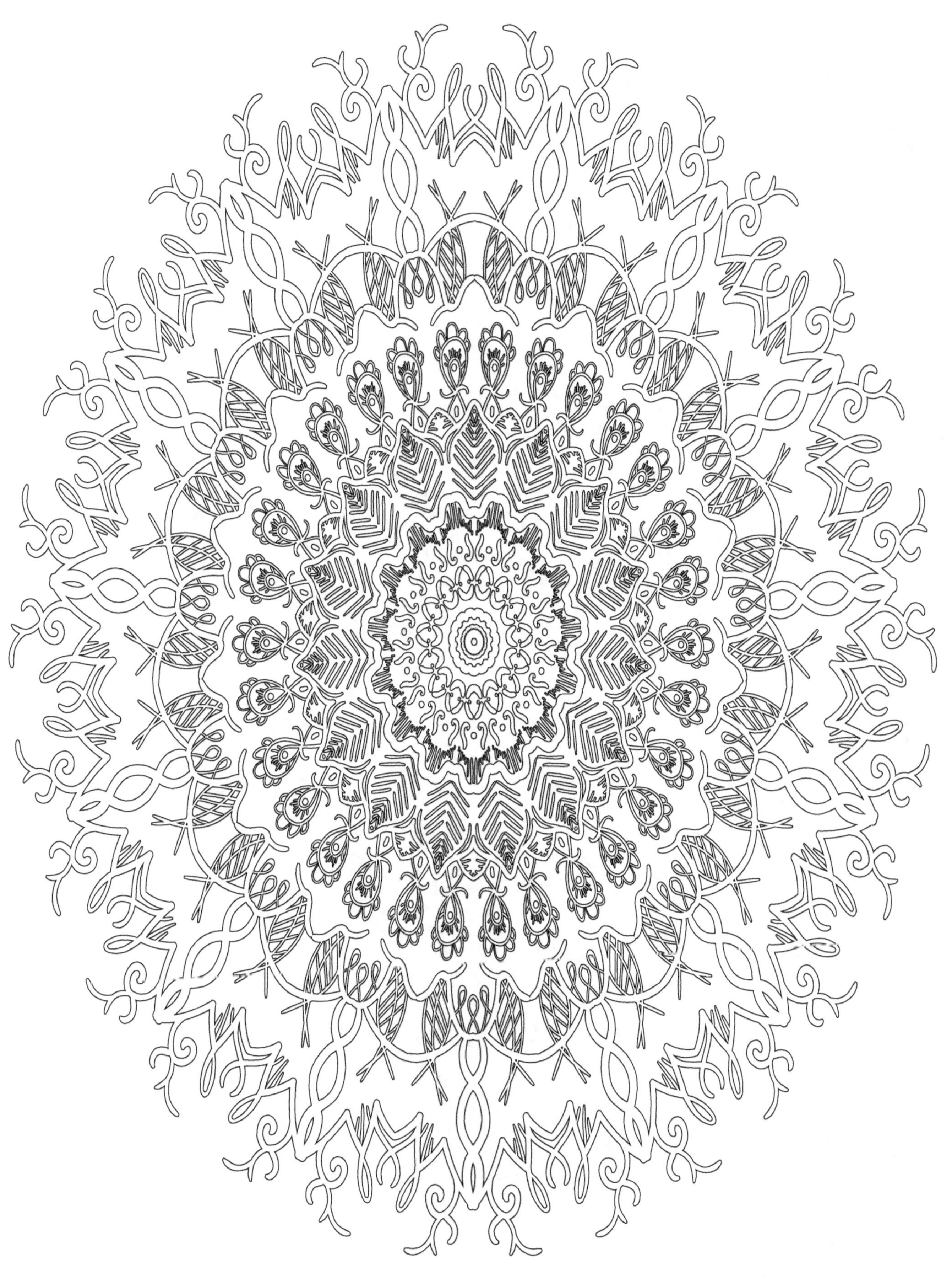

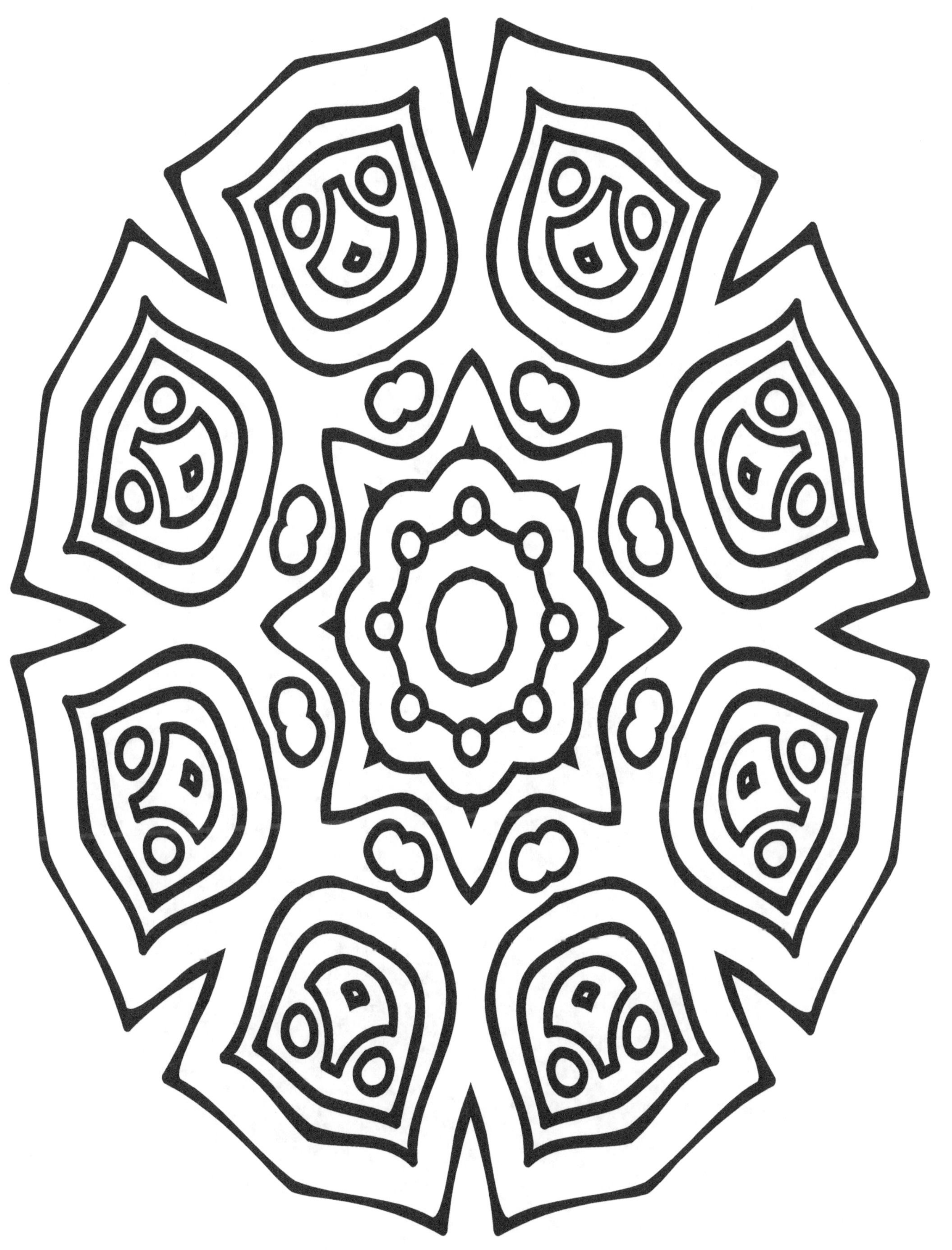

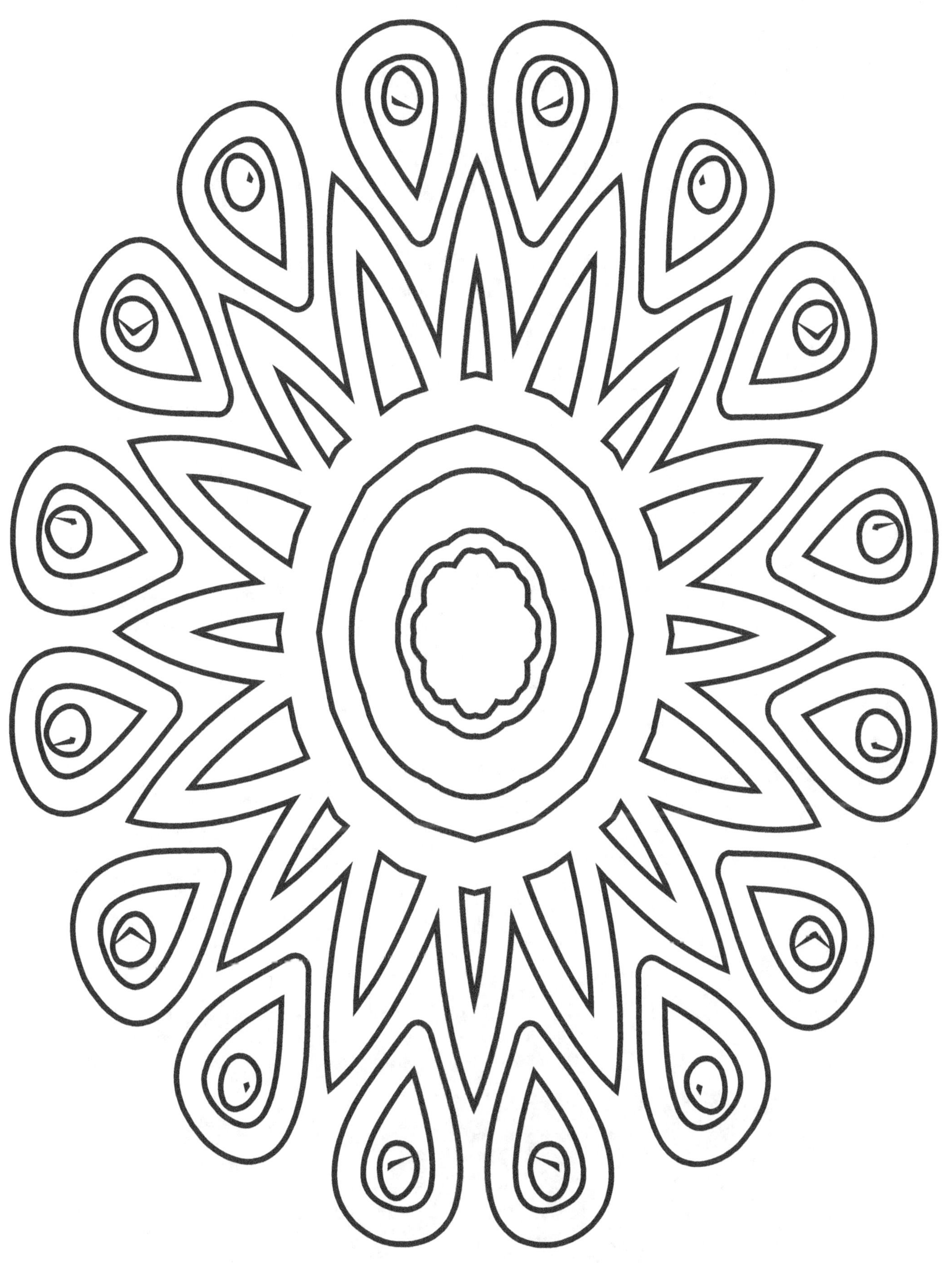

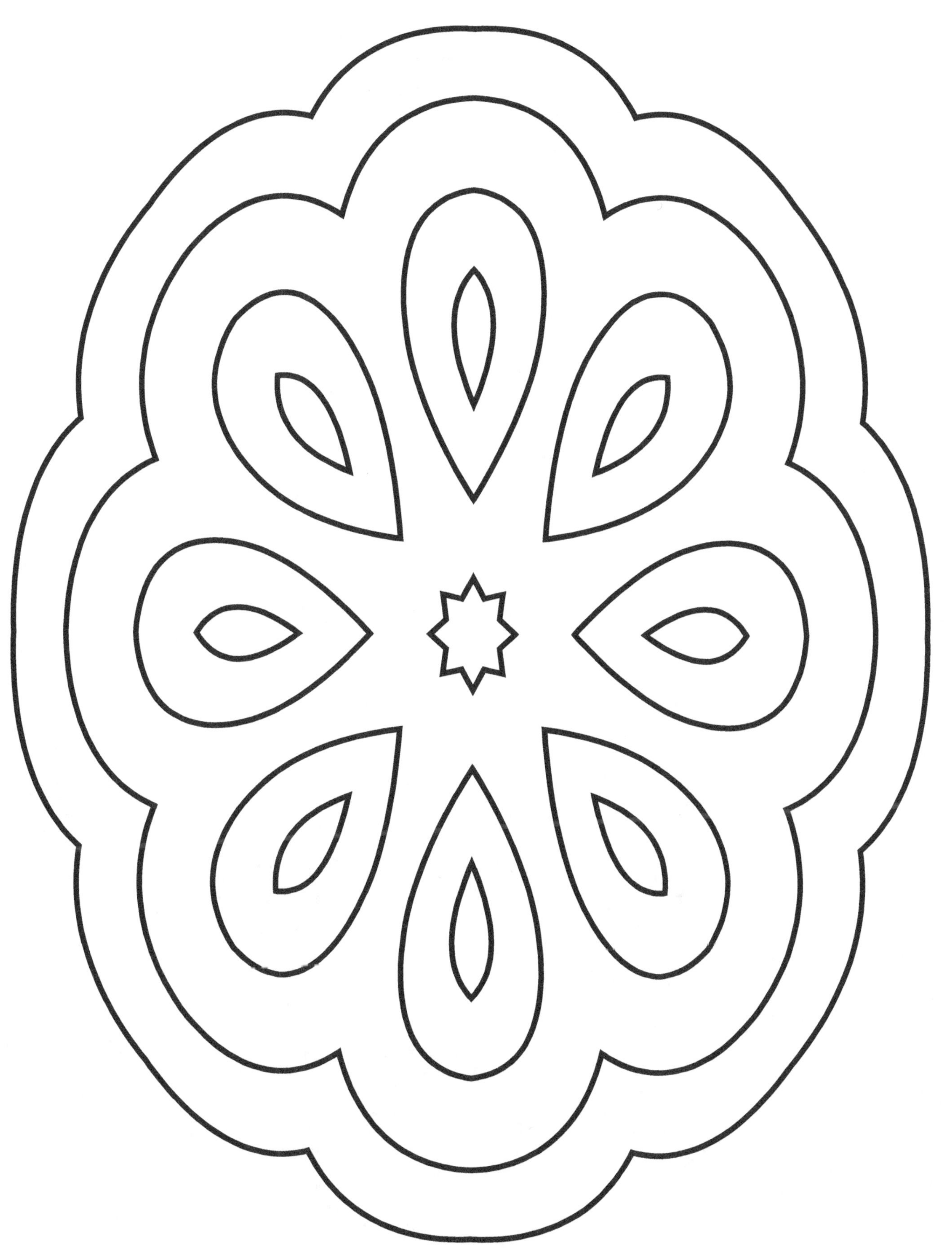

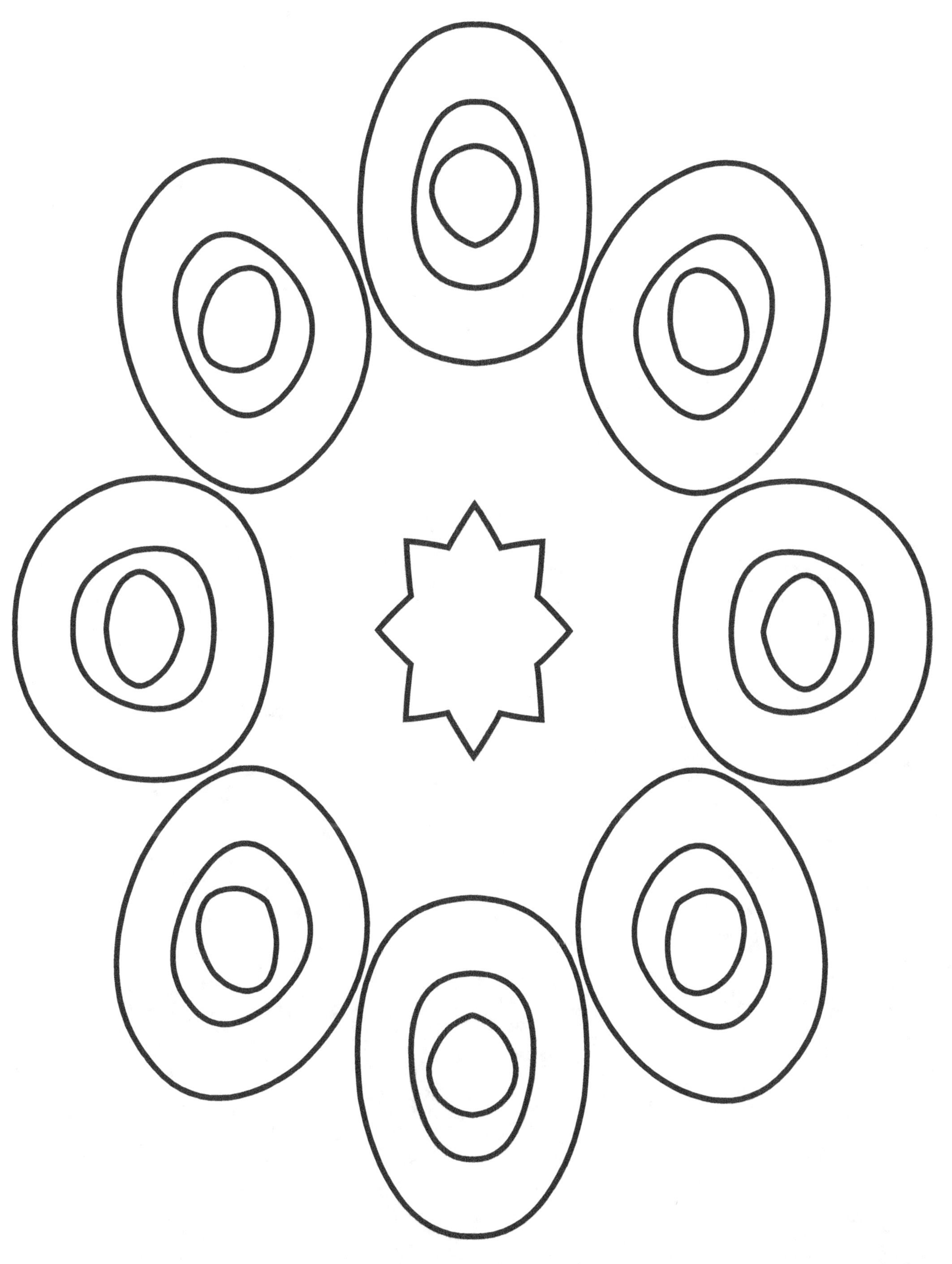

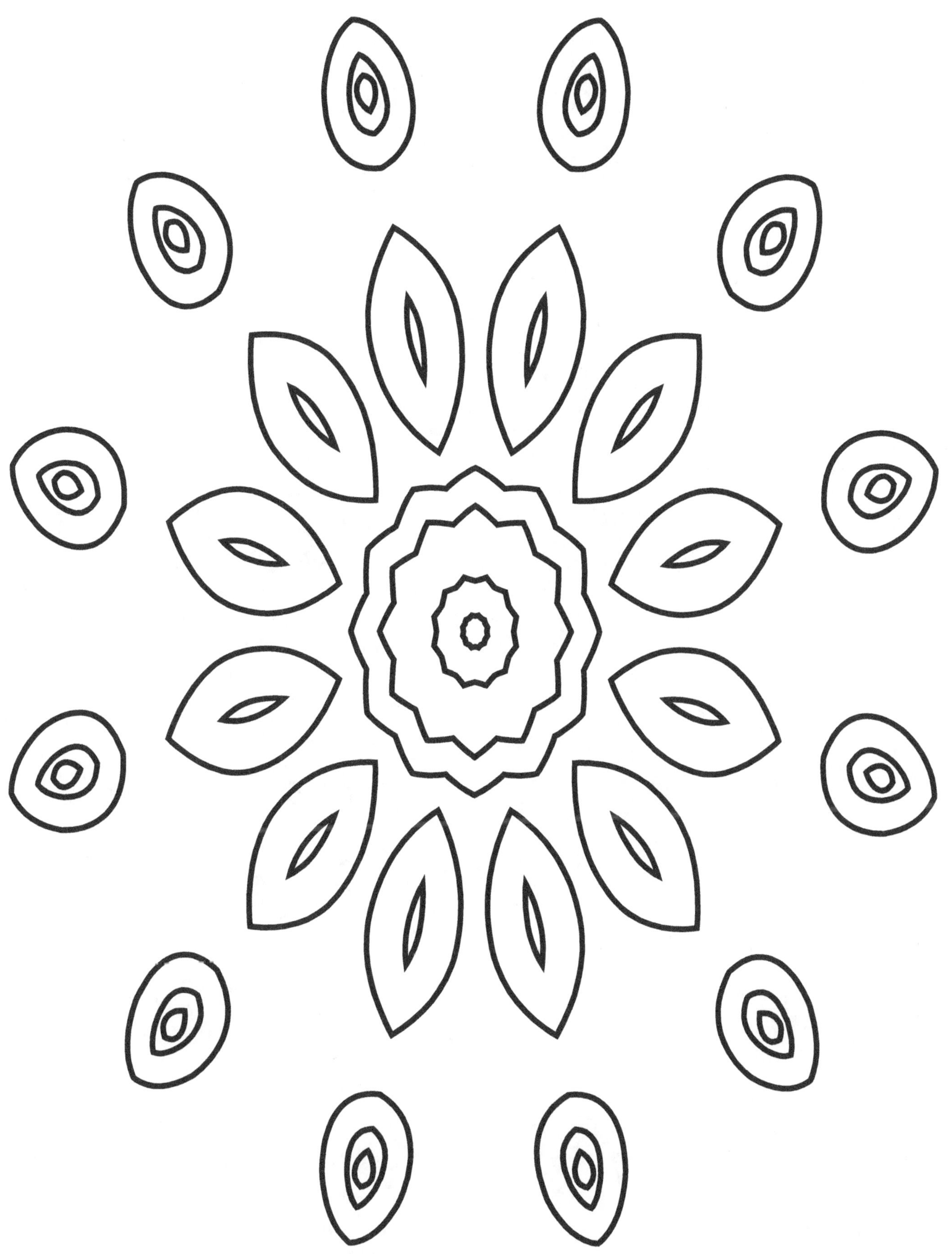

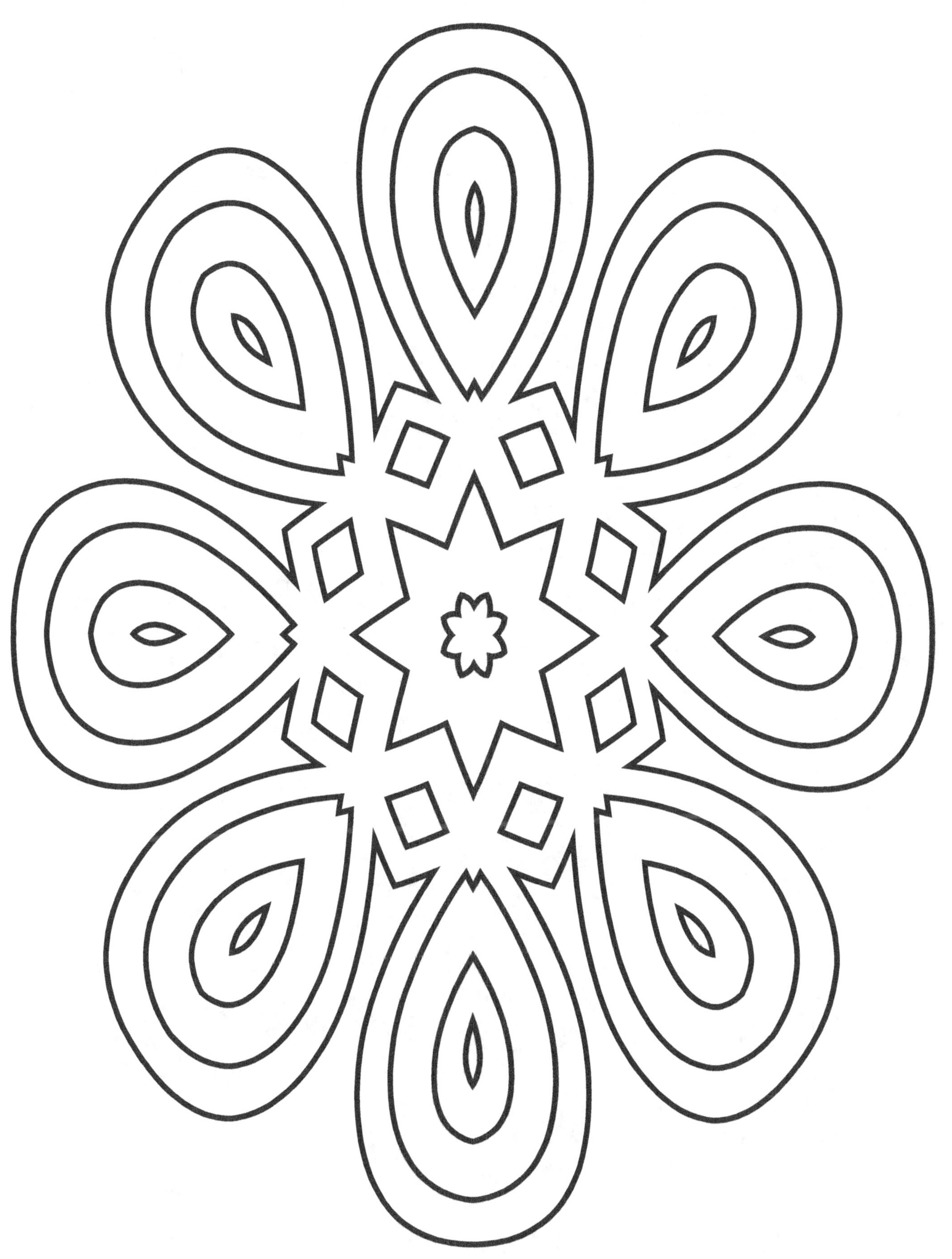

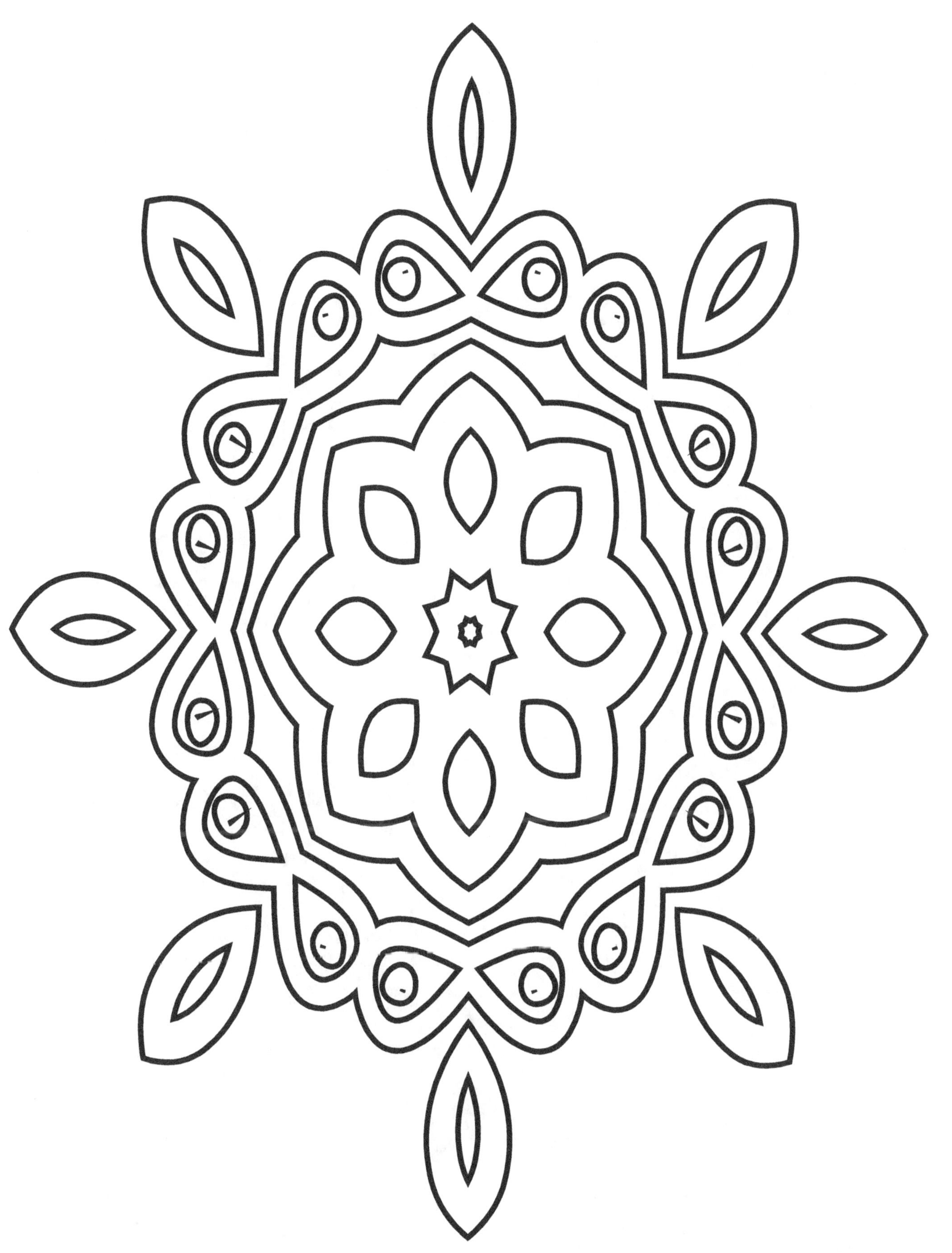

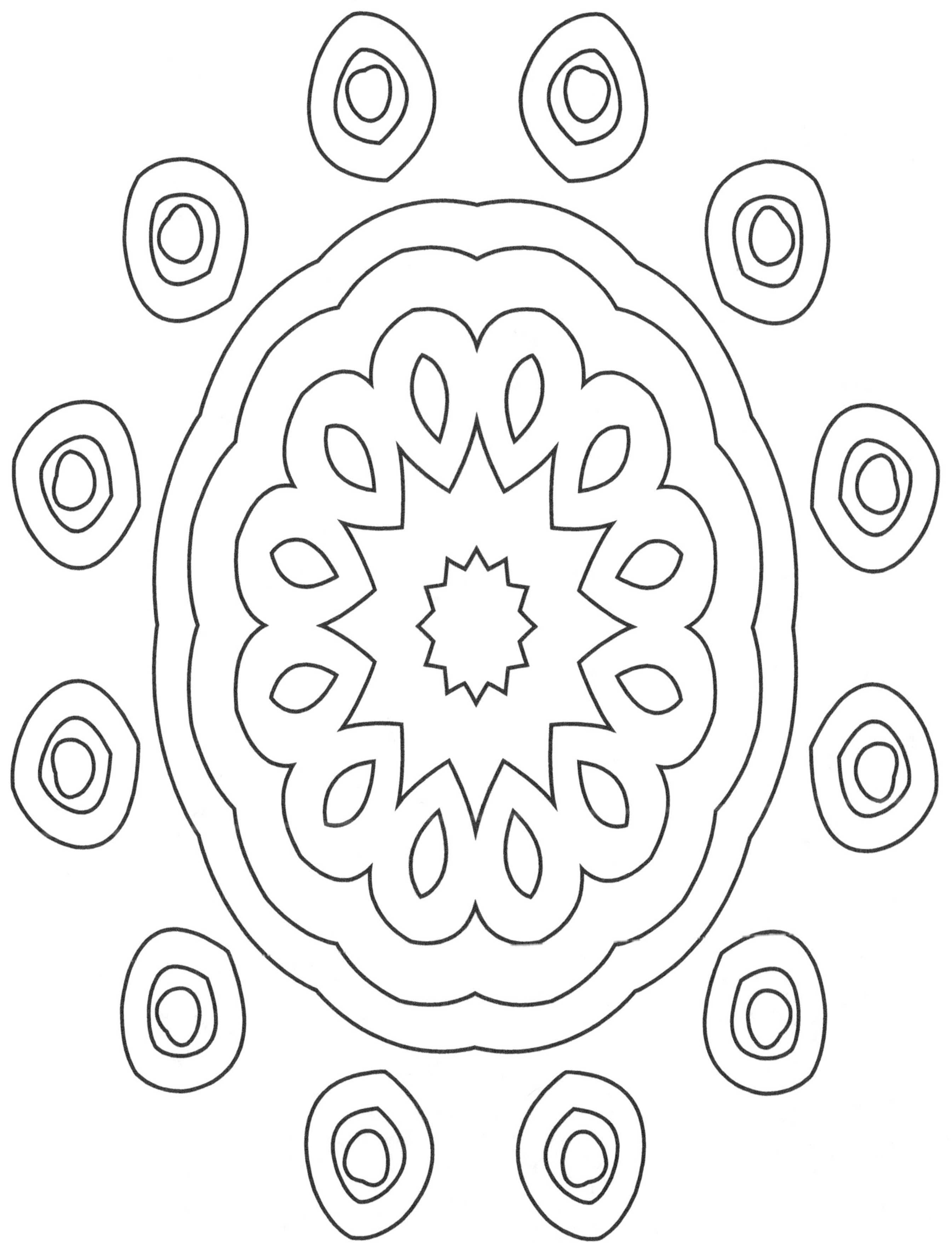

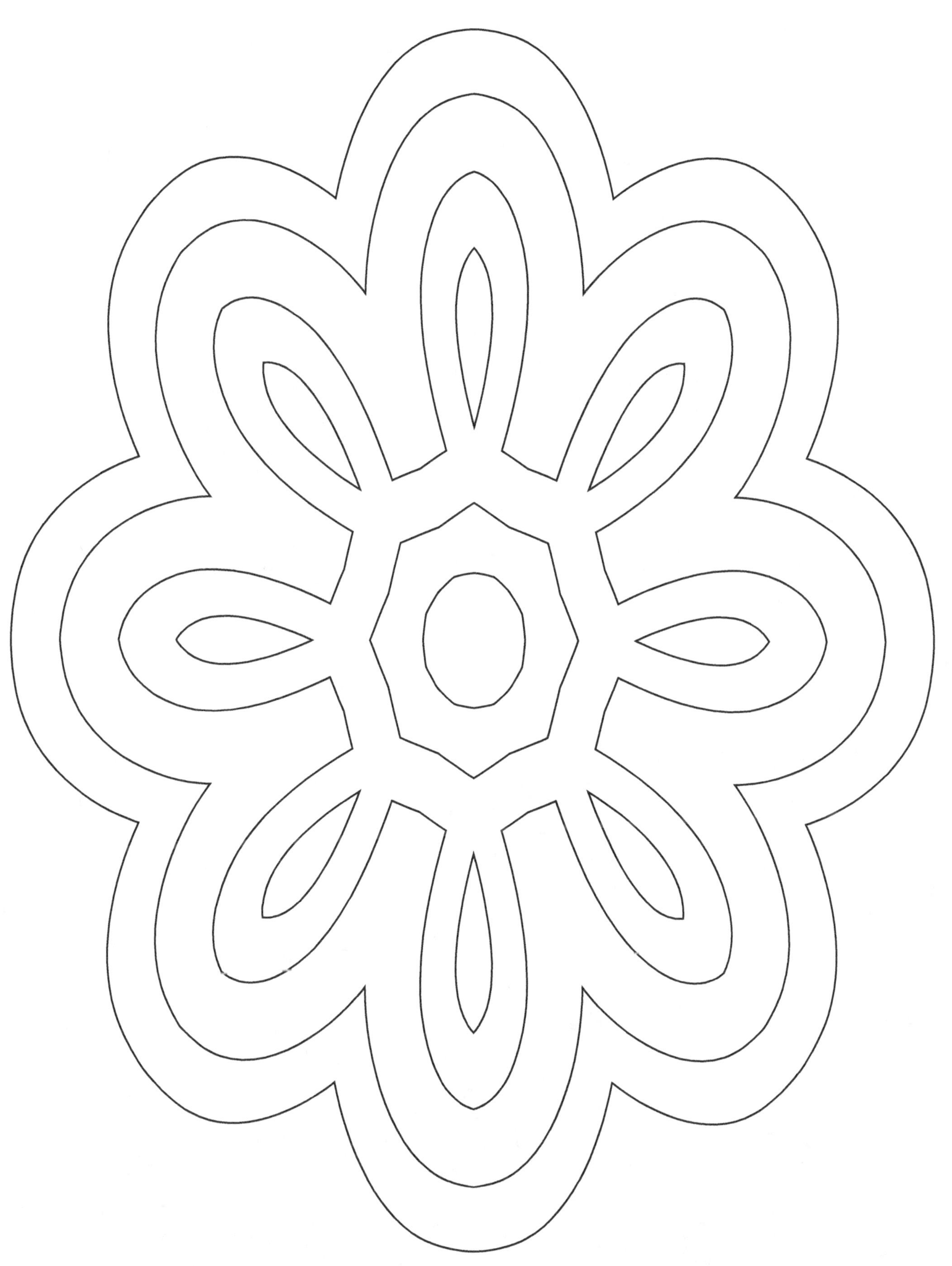

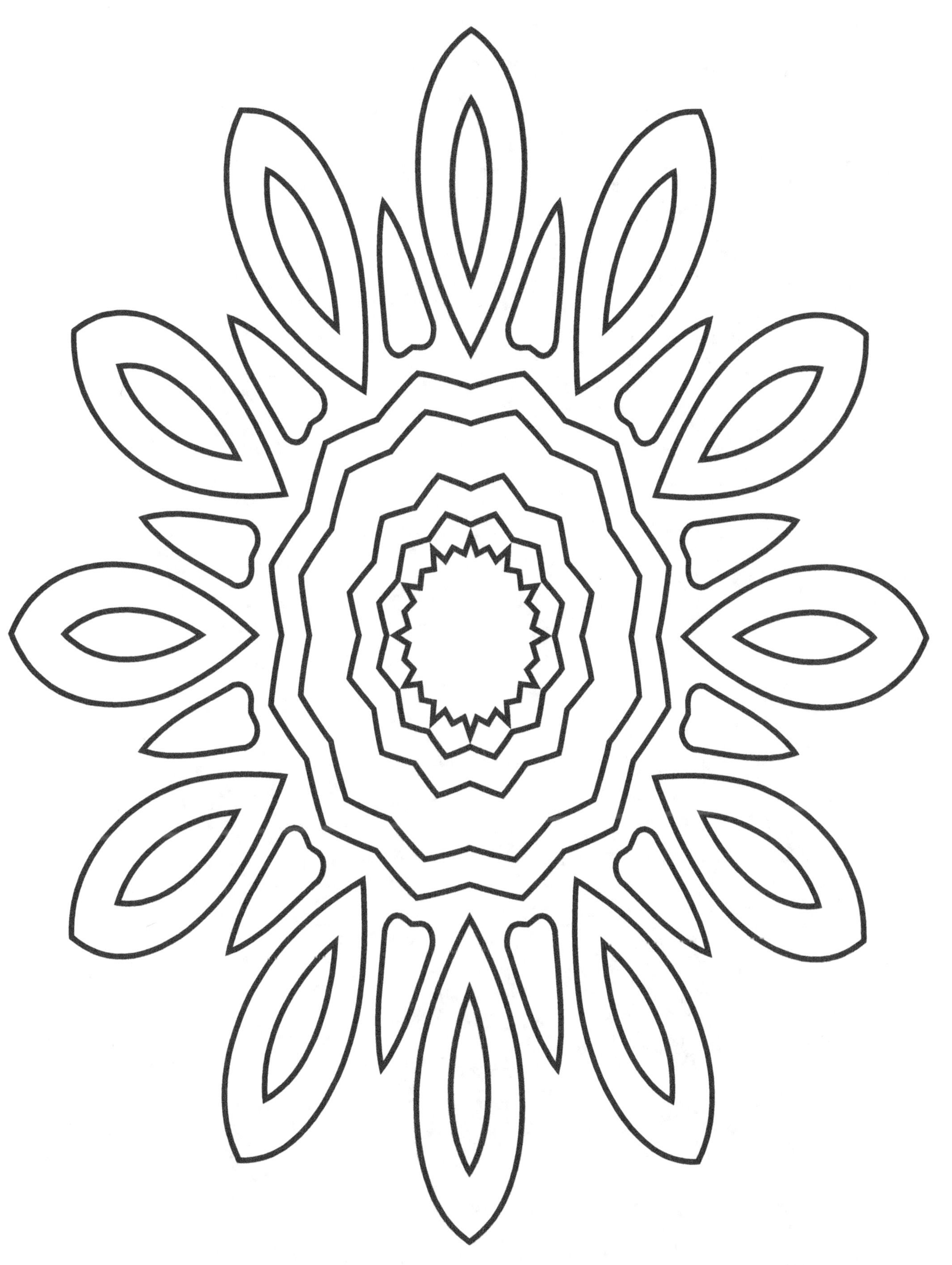

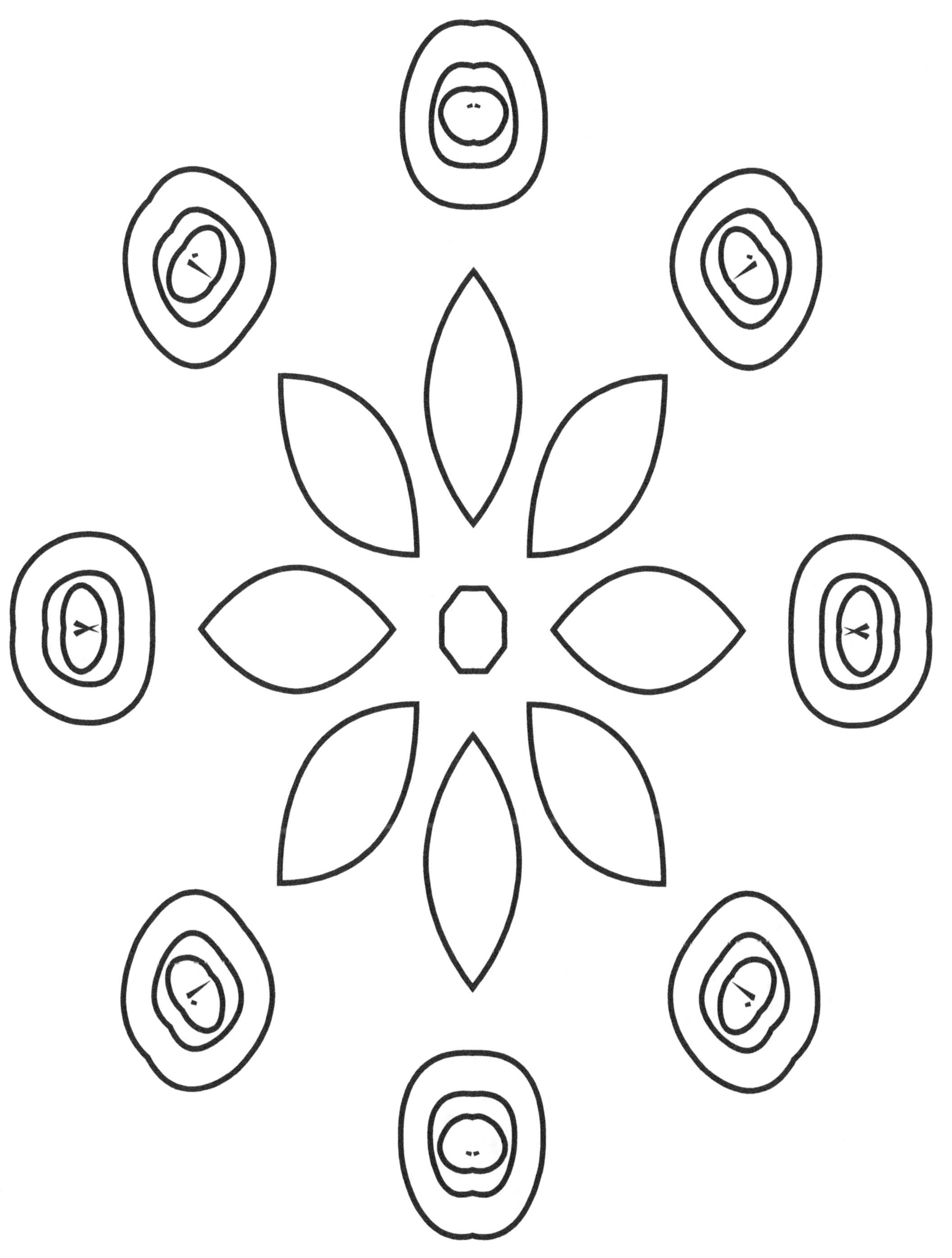

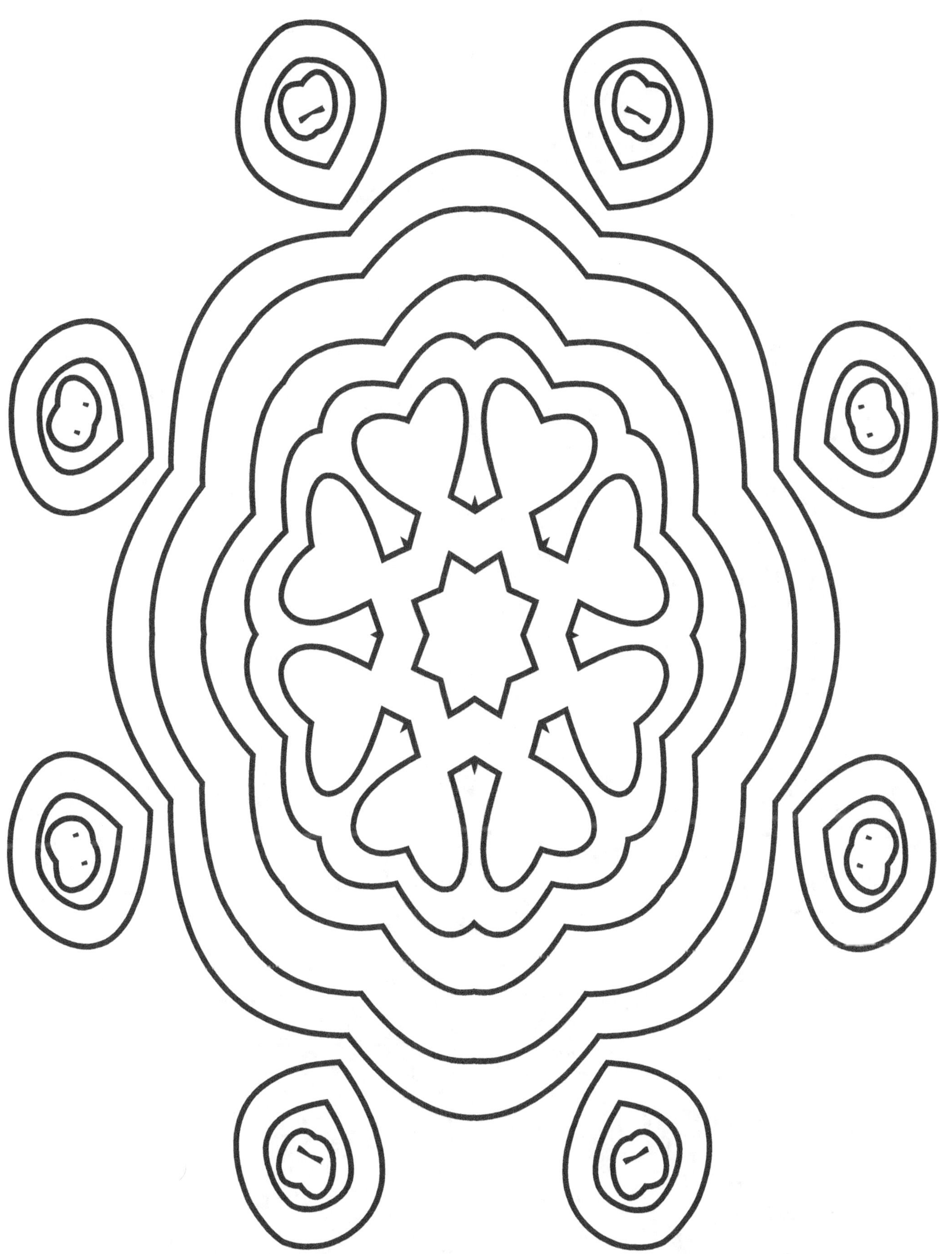

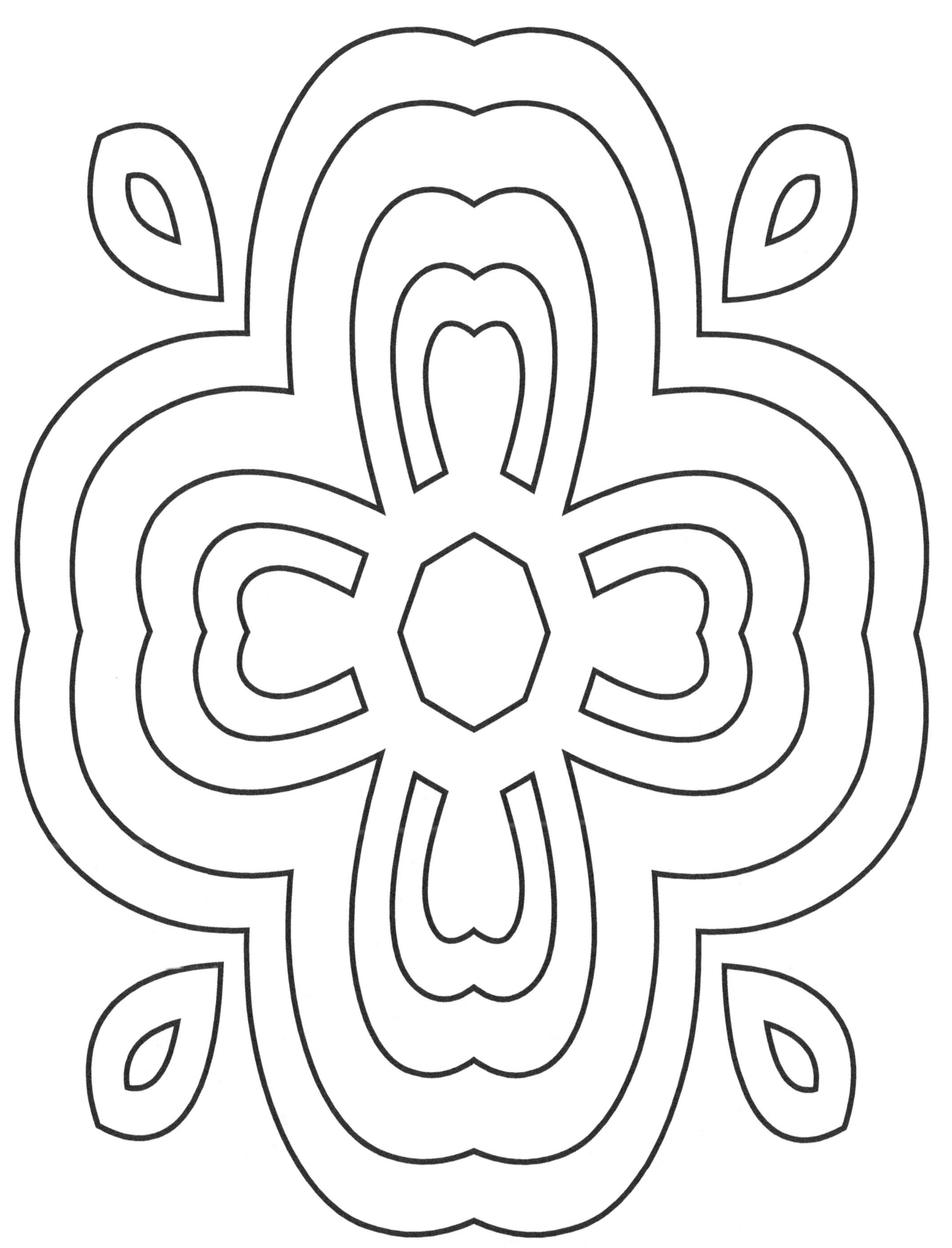

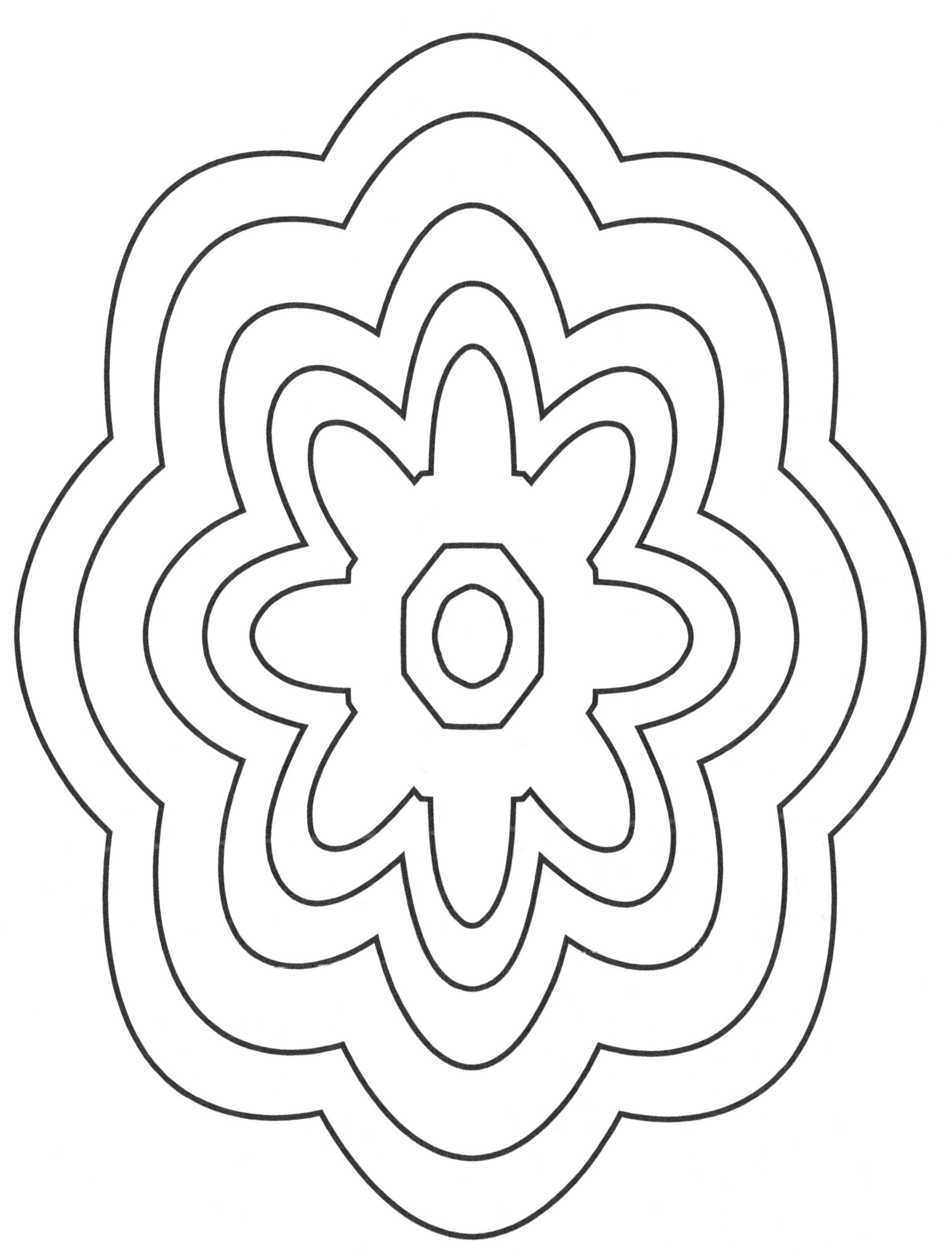

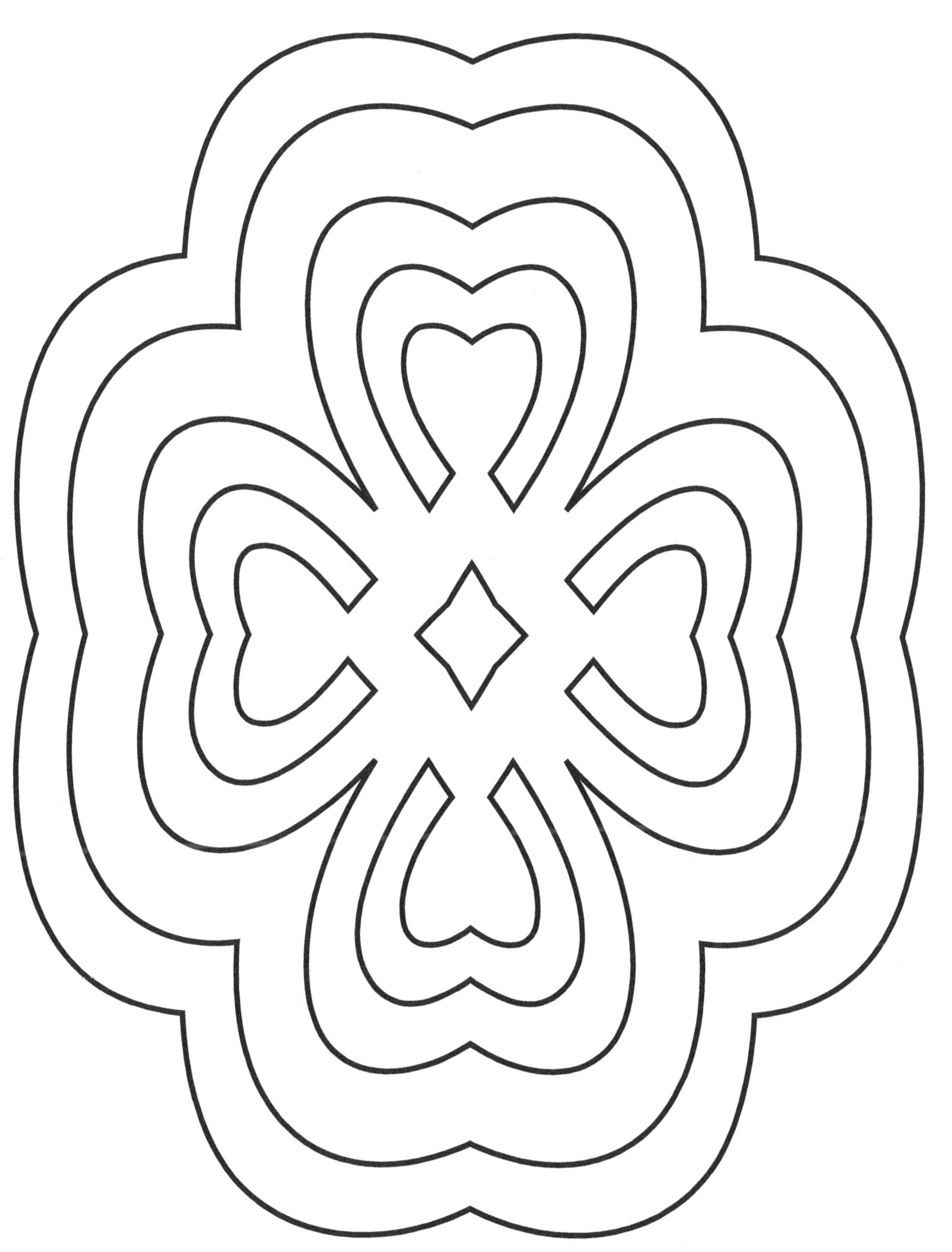

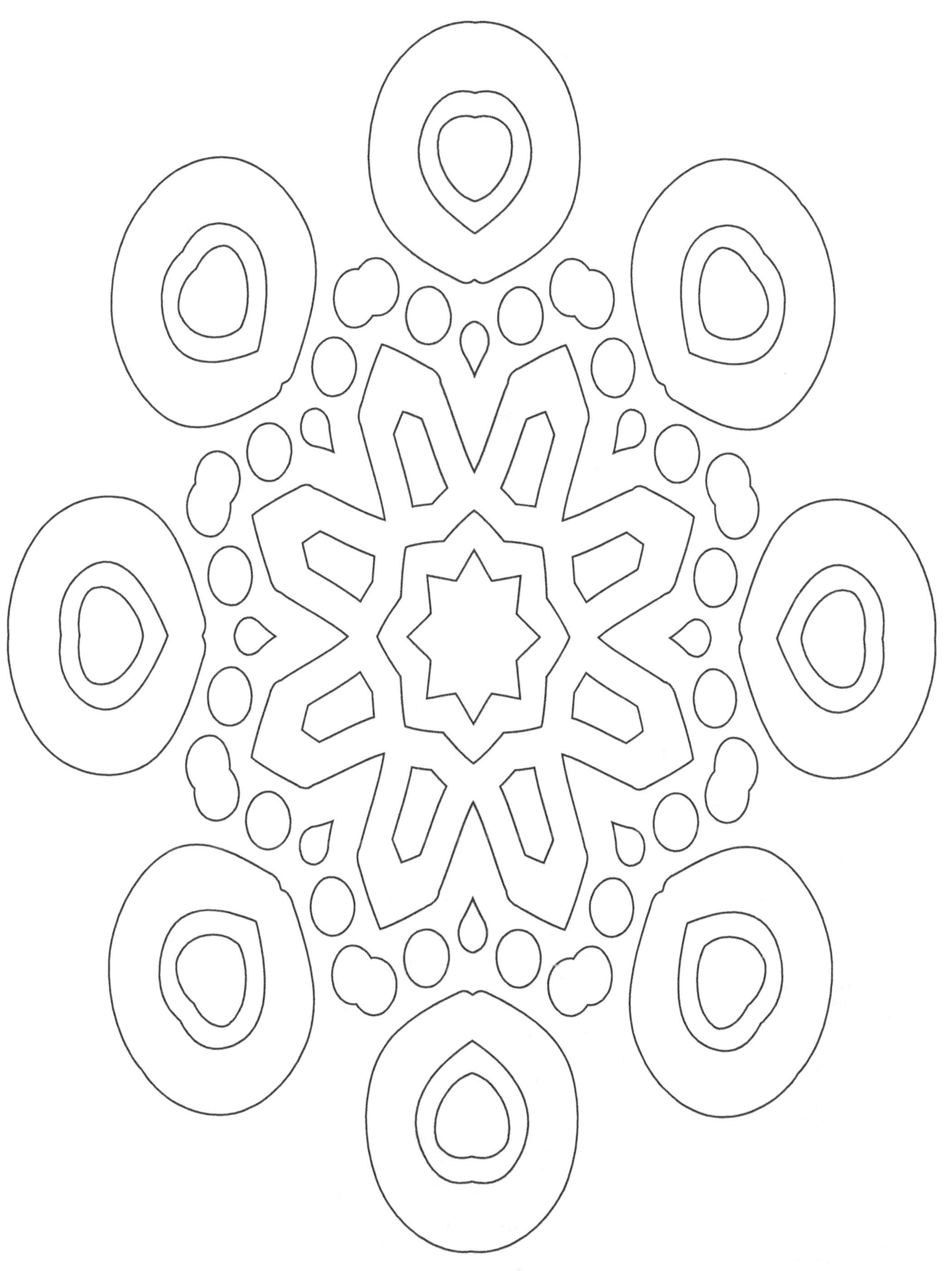

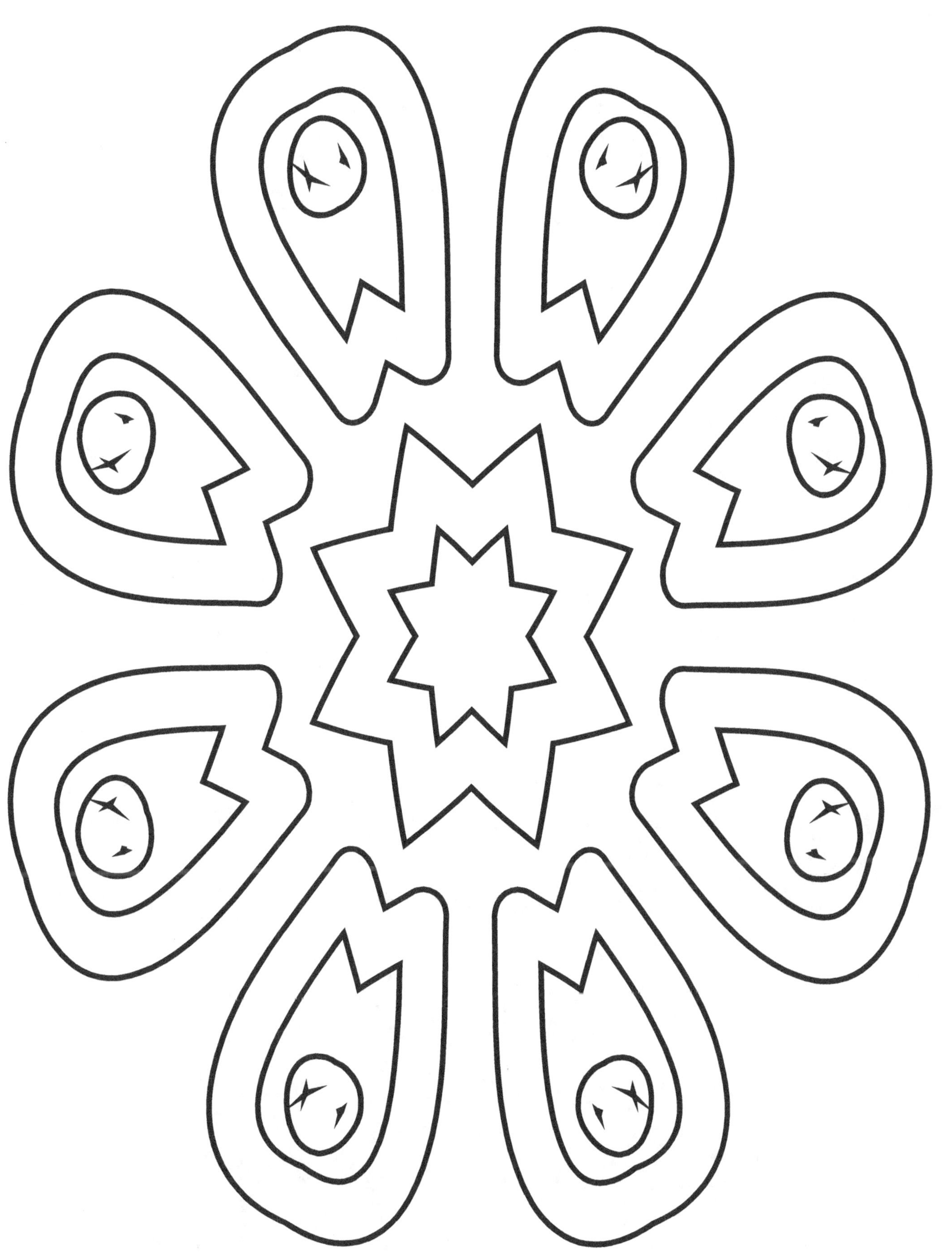

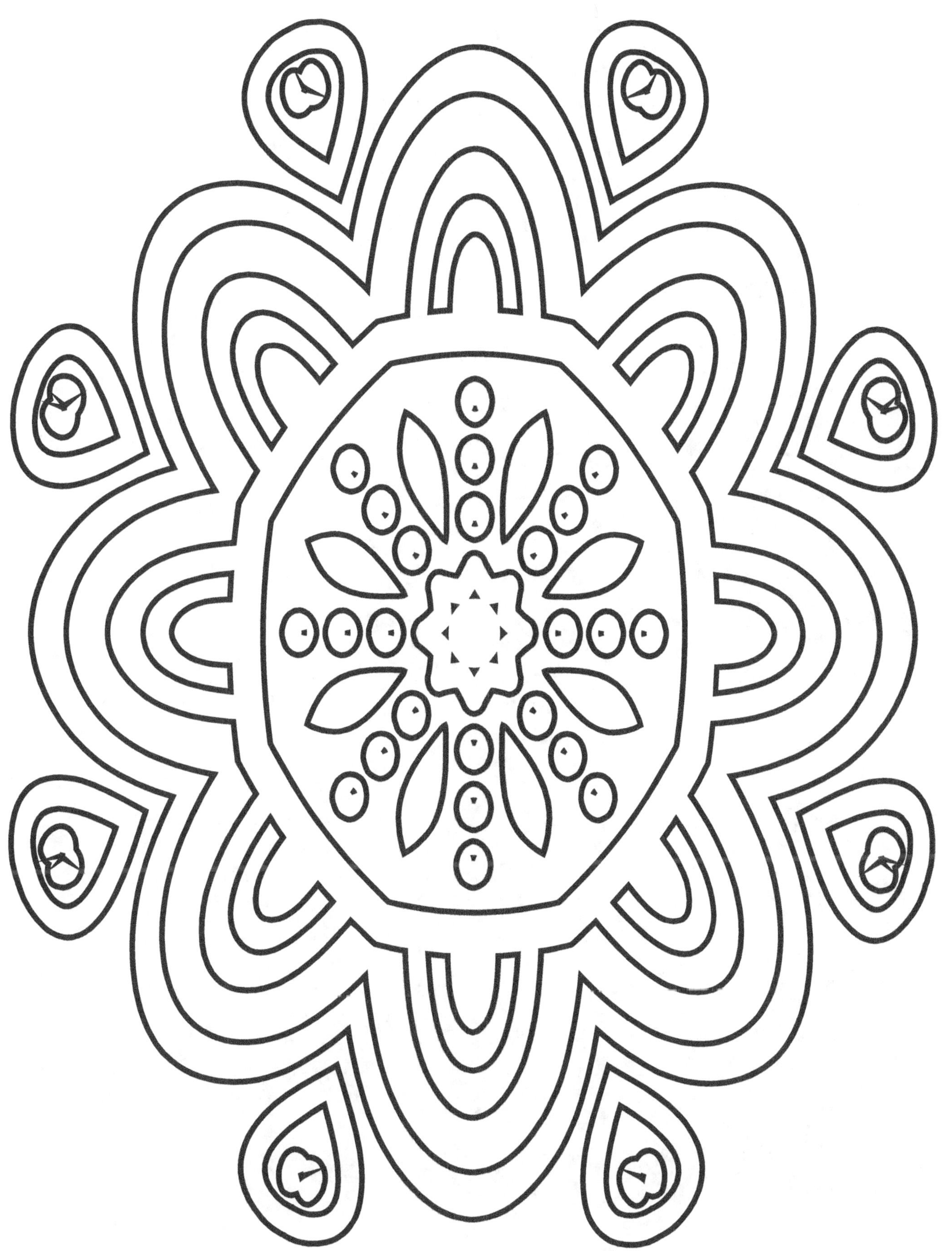

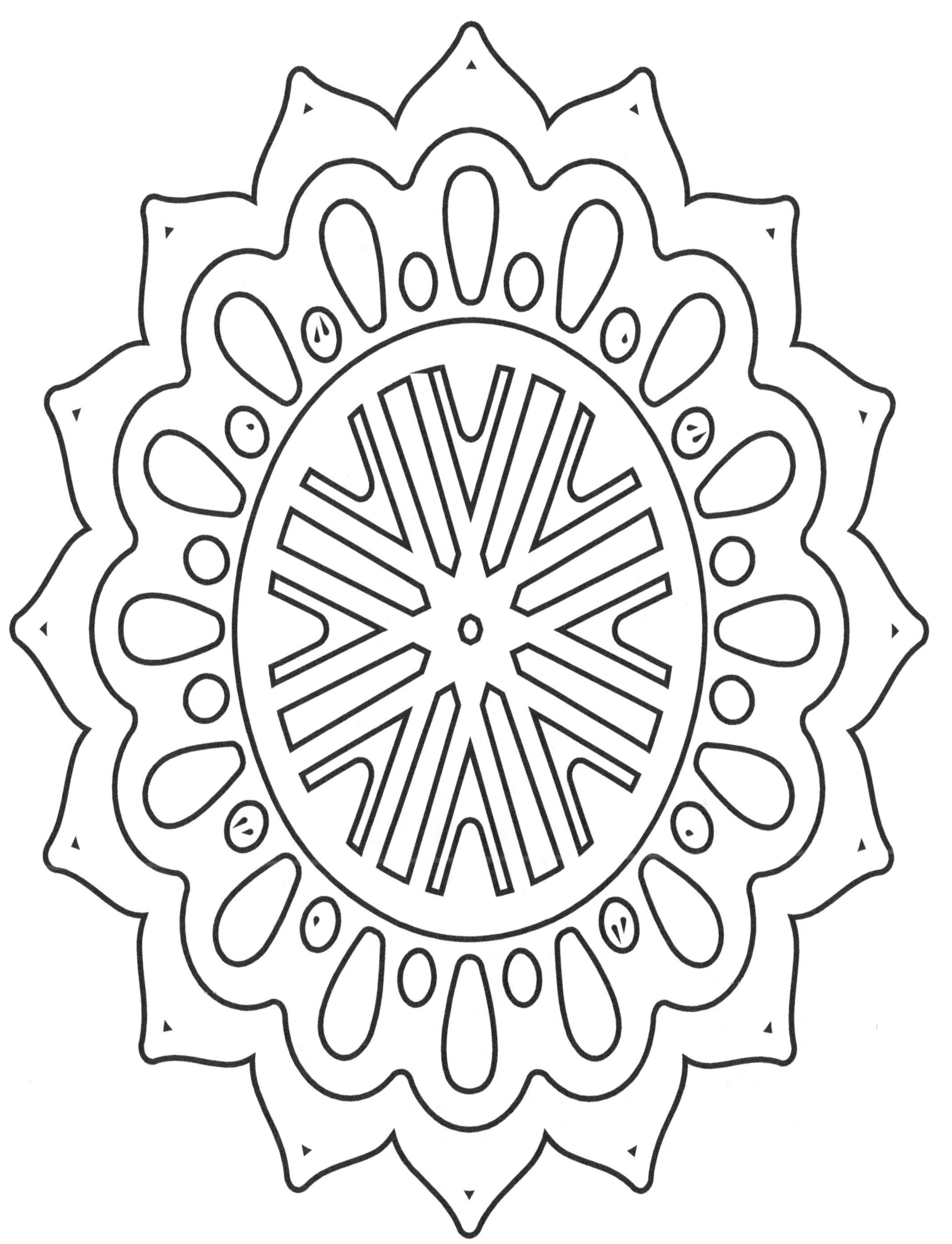

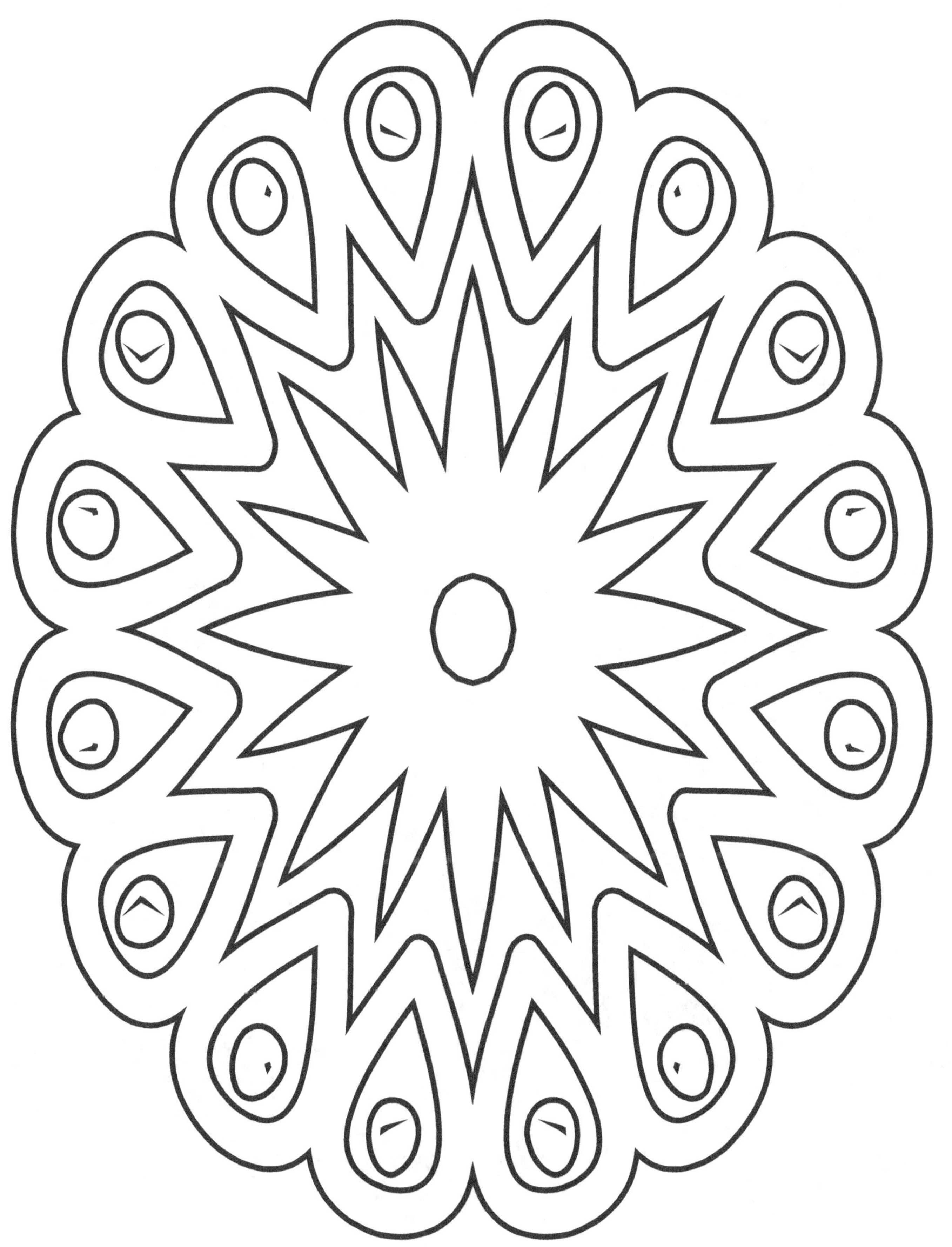

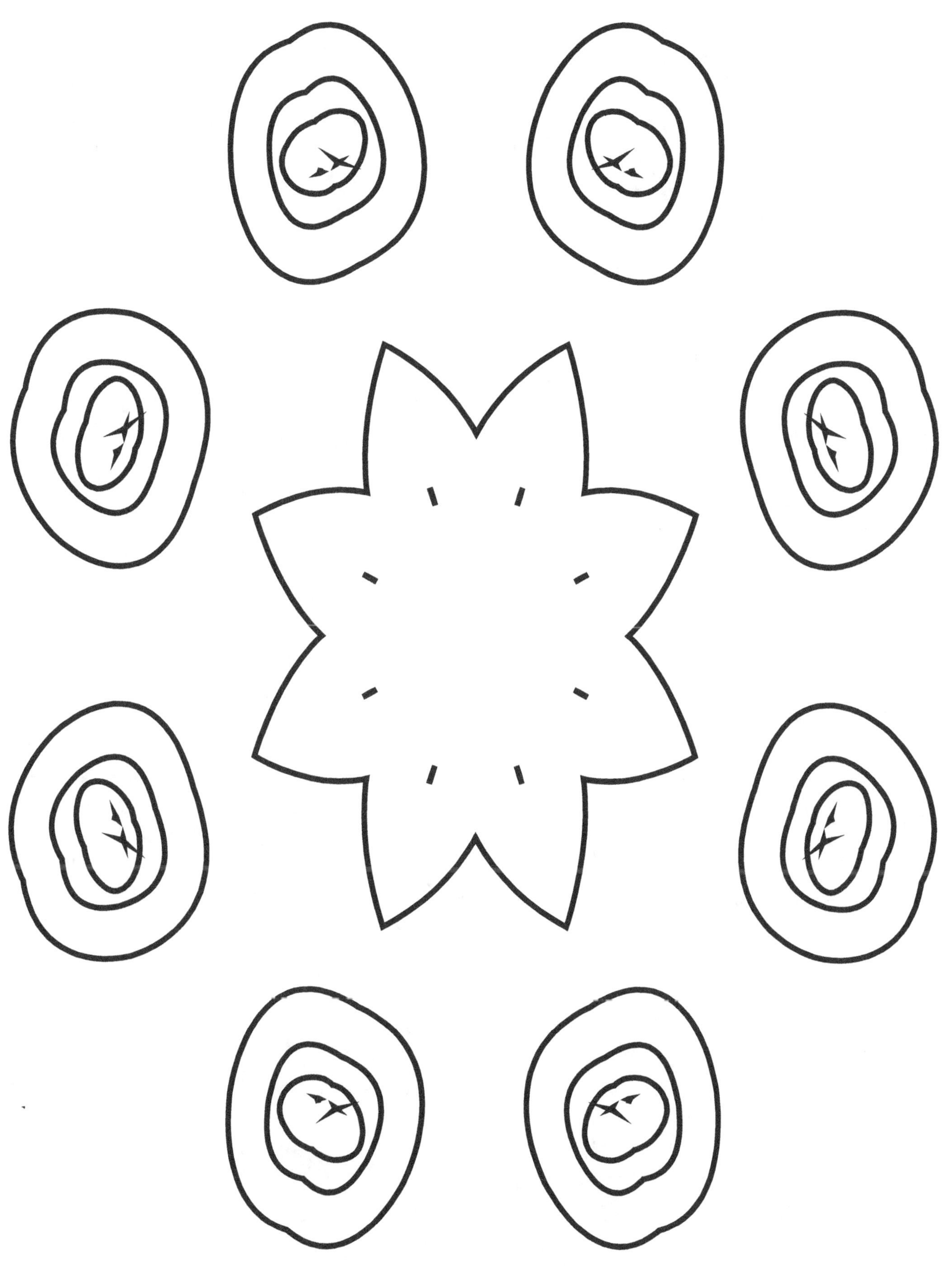